A Christian's Guide to Eating for Health

Janet Mutter, a freelance writer who has a particular interest in nutrition and social issues, is a frequent contributor to *Christian Woman* magazine, with features on food, cooking and the use of herbs. She has travelled widely, and at present lives in Kenya.

Christian Woman Books

Series Editor: Gail Lawther

Creativity
Using your talents
Eileen Mitson and others

Family Planning
The ethics and practicalities
of birth control methods
Gail Lawther

Alone with God
Making the most
of your quiet time
Jean Holl

A Woman's Privilege
Jean Brand

Birthright?
A Christian woman
looks at abortion
Maureen Long

Eating for Health
Janet Mutter

Children under Pressure
Pat Wynnejones

Other titles in preparation

Eating for Health

JANET MUTTER

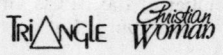

First published 1986
Triangle
SPCK
Holy Trinity Church
Marylebone Road
London NW1 4DU

Copyright © Janet Mutter 1986

All rights reserved. No part of this book may be reproduced or
transmitted in any form or by any means, electronic or
mechanical, including photocopying, recording, or by any
information storage and retrieval system, without permission in
writing from the publisher

ACKNOWLEDGEMENTS

Unless otherwise indicated, biblical quotations are from
the New International Version, © 1973, 1978, 1984,
International Bible Society, and are used by permission.
Biblical quotations marked RSV are from the Revised Standard
Version, copyrighted 1946, 1952, © 1971, 1973 by the Division
of Christian Education of the National Council of the Churches
of Christ in the USA, and are used by permission.
Appendix 1 is from the Department of Health and Social
Security *Report on Health and Social Subjects 15*, and is used
by permission.

British Library Cataloguing in Publication Data

Mutter, Janet
   Eating for health. – (Christian woman books)
   1. Food – Religious aspects – Christianity
   I. Title   II. Series
   261.5'6   TX357

ISBN 0-281-04229-2

Typeset by Input Typesetting Ltd, London
Printed in Great Britain by
Hazel Watson & Viney Limited
Member of the BPCC Group
Aylesbury, Bucks.

Contents

	Acknowledgements	iv
	Series Editor's Foreword	vii
	Introduction	1
1	Stewards of Creation	3
2	Healthy Eating	12
3	Protein Foods	27
4	Energy Foods	37
5	Fats	44
6	Vegetables and Fruit	47
7	Herbs	52
8	Drinks	59
9	Changing to a Wholefood Diet	65
10	Planning and Budgeting a Menu	72
11	Nutrition for Special Situations	82
12	The Meal as a Family Occasion	93

RECIPES

Stocks and Soups	101
Salads	106

Sauces and Dressings	110
Starters	114
Fish	117
Poultry	120
Meat Dishes	124
Vegetarian Dishes	127
Vegetables	131
Puddings and Desserts	134
Breakfast Dishes	137
Packed Lunches	139
Drinks	143
Bread, Scones and Pastry	145
Cakes and Biscuits	148
Yoghurt and Cream Cheese	151

APPENDIX

Recommended daily amounts of food energy and nutrients 152

Series Editor's Foreword

Christian women are developing a new awareness of the way our faith touches every part of our lives. Women who have always lived in a Christian environment are facing up to the important issues in the world around them. Women who have found in Christ a new direction for living are seeking to sort out the problems that are hampering their spiritual growth. And many women are rediscovering joy in using their God-given talents, in their relationships with God and with other people, and in their spiritual lives and worship. *Christian Woman* magazine has been privileged to be part of this learning process.

As a result of this deepening awareness and commitment to Christianity, many books have been published which help women to sort out what God can do for them as women, as wives, as career people, as mothers, as single women. Most of these books however have been rooted in the American culture; this *Christian Woman* series has come into being because we believe it is important that we have books that talk our own language, and are relevant to everyday life in our own culture.

Each book in this series will deal with some aspect of living as a Christian woman in today's world. I am delighted that we have been able to be part of the blossoming of God's church in this way. We hope that the books will help you as a Christian woman to overcome problems, enrich your life and your relationships, learn more of God, think through important issues, enjoy your femininity, make wise choices, and deepen your commitment to Jesus Christ.

In these books we have invited people to share what they have learned about living as Christians. Not everyone will agree with all the ideas expressed in each book, but I know that you will find every book in the series interesting and thought-provoking.

Books change people's lives – perhaps these books will change your life.

GAIL LAWTHER

Introduction

With so many books on healthy eating already in the bookshops, you may be forgiven for asking if we really need another – and a Christian one at that. Has it not all been said before, and can a Christian book really add anything else that can be of use?

I hope so. The general books are fine as far as they go. We should eat properly if we are in a position to do so, because diet affects our health, our outlook on life and our behaviour. And a proper diet is a doubly important consideration for a Christian because our bodies are not our own, they belong to God and are temples of his Holy Spirit (1 Corinthians 6.19). And so it is right that we maintain them by a proper diet and plenty of exercise and sleep. This gives us a healthy mind and body and will deepen our spiritual life so that God can use us more effectively.

Taking this a step further, a healthy body looks good, but looks even better if it is well-groomed and dressed according to our personality and means. We Christians are getting better at this, but we so often neglect our appearance and can look unhealthy and dull. It is such a poor witness to our Lord's bountiful care for us, and was one of the things that put me off Christianity for quite a while before my conversion. I dreaded the thought of turning into what I believed was the mandatory Christian clone, plain and drab. I had seen so many of them that I thought this was the norm! I know differently now, of course, but I still think it is an offence against the God who made us. His taste, colour and beauty are so abundant and varied that we should reflect this imaginativeness in our own appearance and lifestyles – unless specifically called to do otherwise, as some are.

We should not become obsessive about our diet and appearance, though, and let them dominate our lives. We do not need larders full of expensive food or vast wardrobes of costly clothes to reflect God's glory. We can use what he has given us, an adequate diet and a few well-kept clothes with some accessories that suit us, so that beauty is a natural part of our lives.

To return to my original point, secular books do not go far enough for the Christian because our responsibility does not end with caring for ourselves; we are also responsible for one another and for the rest of God's creation. So any Christian book on healthy eating has to acknowledge this fact and suggest ways of satisfying the needs of others as well as our own needs, without harming the environment. That is what I hope to do.

1

Stewards of Creation

Stewardship is a word we use in connection with money, time and possessions, but we do not often use it with regard to nature. Some explain this by arguing that creation is rarely mentioned in the New Testament and so it need not concern us. This is not so. Jesus came to fulfil the Law, not to abolish it (Matthew 5.17–18). He was preaching to Jews who already knew the Law and it was unnecessary to repeat it. Jesus was concerned with salvation, but that did not invalidate man's responsibility for the well-being of all creation.

This responsibility towards creation is well documented in the Old Testament. It shows man's unique position as both a distinct and an integral part of nature – a situation that has not changed today.

Man is distinct from the rest of creation because he was the only creature made in God's image and was, therefore, the pinnacle of God's creation (Genesis 1.26). He was given the land to work and care for (Genesis 2.15) and authority to 'Rule over the fish of the sea and the birds of the air and over every living creature that moves on the ground' (Genesis 1.28). As a sign of his sovereignty over them, Adam was asked by God to name the animals (Genesis 2.19–20).

Although man had a unique and powerful position in creation it did not mean that he could govern as he liked. The Old Testament meaning of the world 'rule' implies stewardship and care, not ownership. Rulers during the Old

Testament period were well aware that the world and everything in it belonged to God (Psalm 24.1) and they were given authority by God to rule in a way that satisfied the needs of all living creatures without harming them.

Man is also an integral part of creation and has his definite place in the life on this planet. This is graphically illustrated in Psalm 104.

> The moon marks off the seasons,
>   and the sun knows when to go down.
> You bring darkness, it becomes night,
>   and all the beasts of the forest prowl.
> The lions roar for their prey
>   and seek their food from God.
> The sun rises, and they steal away;
>   they return and lie down in their dens.
> Then man goes out to his work,
>   to his labour until evening.
>   (Psalm 104.19–23)

You notice that the psalmist slots man in below the lions, not because man is less important than they are, but to show that in the rhythm of creation, every creature, including man, has his own time, place and purpose on earth, as part of a whole. God satisfies the needs of every creature. He gives them water, food and places to live and sets them to live out their lives in harmony and interdependence with the earth and each other. Today the natural sciences are discovering just how important that harmony and interdependence is for the well-being of the planet. It seems there is a fine balance in creation and what affects one creature will affect them all sooner or later. So although man is distinct from nature, he is inextricably linked with it and needs the balance in nature to function properly as a human. Man cannot live without it.

But, as we know, the Fall destroyed that harmony. Once man disobeyed God and went his own way, he became separated from God, lost God's perspective and, as a result, lost his proper relationship with his fellows and with creation. The land became hostile and gave up its fruit grudgingly: 'Cursed is the ground because of you; through painful toil you will eat of it all the days of your life' (Genesis 3.17). And the animal kingdom treated us as enemies: 'The fear and dread of you will fall upon all the beasts of the earth and all the birds of the air, upon every creature that moves along the ground, and upon all the fish of the sea' (Genesis 9.2).

As time has gone on and our separation from God has become greater, we have, one way or another, done increasing damage to the environment, to the extent that many now believe that Isaiah's prophecy, 'The earth lies polluted under its inhabitants' (Isaiah 24.5, RSV) was for our time.

Many areas of environmental concern lie outside the scope of this book, but food production does not; it affects us all. It is salutary to see how we are unwittingly damaging ourselves, our neighbours and creation by the way in which we obtain our food.

Ourselves
We will have a closer look at the rights and wrongs of diet in the next chapter, but it is worth mentioning here that nearly 40 per cent of our population is overweight and, despite medical advances, doctors' waiting rooms are as full as they ever were, but now largely with cases of food-assisted diseases such as heart disease and bowel problems, caused by over-eating the wrong kinds of food. It is interesting to see how nutritionists are beginning to confirm the truth of biblical teaching about food. They tell us that we should eat more fibre, because our digestive systems are designed to take it. This is confirmed in Genesis 1.29 because when God gave man seed-bearing plants and fruits to eat (he added meat and everything else after the flood [Genesis 9.3]) he gave us a high fibre diet!

The Land

God knew that the land was a living organism and, like every creature, needed food and rest in order to thrive. So he built these requirements into the Mosaic laws in the form of the law about the sabbatical year which stipulated that every seven years the land was to lie fallow for a year (Leviticus 25.3–4). God promised that the Israelites would live in safety and plenty if they obeyed these laws (Leviticus 25.18–19). Unfortunately these laws are disregarded in the West today.

It is true that there is no shortage of food in the West, but it is at a cost to our environment. Since the last war our farms have produced an abundance and variety of food unequalled at any other time. Production is so great that £5,000 million, half the EEC annual agricultural budget, is spent on storage and disposal of surplus foods. We have grain and butter mountains and wine lakes and in 1984 destroyed thousands of tonnes of fruit and vegetables to protect food prices. How do we do it? By high-tech. farming, which is geared to high yields, dependent upon chemicals and encouraged by EEC subsidies, chemical producers and farm machinery manufacturers.

In arable farming, for instance, instead of the usual crop rotation, many farms specialise in mono-agriculture, growing one crop year after year in the same field and relying heavily on chemical fertilisers and pesticides to keep production high and reduce the diseases that occur when land has no rest or change.

The financial incentives in high-tech. farming are radically altering our landscape and in many parts of the country small fields with hedges are being replaced by huge cornfields that ripple over the horizon, making parts of Britain look like the Canadian prairies. During the last forty years it is estimated that 60 per cent of lowland heath has been lost under the plough; along with 50 per cent and more of ancient woodland; 95 per cent of herb-rich meadow; 50 per cent of lowland fen and mire and 80 per cent of lowland sheep walks. And that is not to mention the countless miles of hedgerows that have been dug up, all of which have led to the destruction of food and habitats for animals, plants and insects, many of which are now bordering on extinction. When did you last see a bank of primroses or a field full of cowslips? They were quite common when I was a child and that was not *so* long ago, but these flowers are becoming as rare as orchids now. Many plants and creatures that do escape the plough are often caught by chemical sprays, and this has resulted in a serious loss of wildlife in some areas.

The benefits of this type of farming are short-lived, and for reasons that include over-production, soil erosion and soil compaction by heavy machinery, the beginnings of desertification have already set in in some arable areas so that ever-increasing amounts of chemical fertiliser are needed to maintain high yields.

Animal Farming
There have been revolutionary changes in this area too. We get chickens from egg to oven within forty-five days, instead of eighteen weeks, and cattle are ready for slaughter within fourteen months instead of the usual four years. These incredible figures are at the expense of the traditional, and more humane, methods of farming. Domestic animals have become commodities on many farms. The farmyard chicken pecking in the hedgerows is a thing of the past. Chickens are now reared factory-fashion in small wire cages lining huge, warm, brightly lit battery sheds where their growth and health is maintained by growth hormones and antibiotics. Sheep are increasingly bred to produce three lamb crops every two years instead of two, while more and more cattle are raised in their stalls instead of in the pasture and fed expensive high-energy grain feed instead of inexpensive grass. It takes between 10 and 20 lb of grain to produce 1 lb of meat and for this reason alone it is easy to sympathise and identify with vegetarians who protest at the indignity to animals reared under these conditions and the use of

grain in this way when millions are starving.

Market Gardening
Commercial growers are also enjoying a boom and there has never been a greater variety of fruit and vegetables for us to choose from. Even vegetables like aubergines and capsicums, once only eaten on foreign holidays, are now home grown and commonplace. The vegetables are large, colourful and look healthy. The market gardener can pride himself on increased yields, reaping 100 tonnes of tomatoes where he once reaped 20 tonnes. How is it done? With chemicals. A recent survey carried out by the Association of Public Analysts shows that a third of all fresh fruit and vegetables on sale in Britain contains chemical residues, including DDT which is banned by the Ministry of Agriculture.

A great deal of food today, whether it is grain, meat or vegetable, is believed to contain traces of chemicals and no one is really certain of the effect these are having on our health. Some investigations do show that chemicals can accumulate in the body and are linked with allergies and illnesses, including some types of cancer.

Our neighbours
As we alter our landscape we are encouraging Third World countries to do the same and instead of producing their own food they are growing cash crops like coffee and meat for export in order to pay off the loans from funding agencies. One example of this is Brazil, home of the world's largest spread of tropical rain forest, the Amazon jungle. This provides 40 per cent of the world's oxygen and home for nearly half the world's plant and animal species. Yet it is being cut down at the rate of fifty acres a minute (or the size of East Germany a year), partly to resettle a growing landless population, but mainly to rear low grade cattle for export, which end up as steaks in American fast food shops and corned beef in Britain and Europe.

The tragic thing is that everyone, including the Brazilian government, knows that tropical rain forest land cannot be put to alternative use. Within seven years of clearing the land it becomes infertile and eventually turns to desert. The jungle does not grow back. Of the 2.5 million hectares cleared during the 1960s and 1970s more than half a million (the size of Switzerland) has been abandoned and more is following.

Yet the Brazilian government can see no other way of solving its economic and social problems. Under pressure from the growing ecology lobby it is protecting pockets of forest, but these are unlikely to be large enough to prevent the changes in climate and rainfall that are already taking place in Brazil.

In the same year that we destroyed much of our surplus food or sold it off cheaply to other developed countries, 10,000 people died each day from starvation, whilst another 800 million lived in complete destitution. None of us can be ignorant of this fact any more after the harrowing news coverage of the famine in sub-Saharan Africa, and especially in Ethiopia where thousands died from starvation when the local harvests failed as a result of overgrazing, poor farming techniques, indiscriminate tree felling, civil war and seven years of drought. But poverty and malnutrition are still a problem, even when there is food, and in some countries 70 per cent of the pre-school children suffer from a protein deficiency which often results in mental retardation and even death.

God has great compassion for the poor and the Mosaic laws were designed to make sure that the poorest person in the community was cared for and provided for by those who had plenty. 'There will always be poor people in the land. Therefore I command you to be open-handed towards . . . the poor and needy in your land' (Deuteronomy 15.11).

The developed world has responded wonderfully to some recent appeals for food and aid. But we need to continue giving over a longer period to appropriate and culturally relevant projects to try to combat the problems in the Third World. Relief is a requirement, not an act of charity. The poor have a right to receive it.

We have obviously strayed a long way from the original principles of stewardship, which were intended to supply the needs of every creature. The wealth gap between the North and South is widening and we are using rapacious farming techniques to satisfy our greed rather than our need, with little thought for the poor, the land, future generations, or of the well-being of other forms of life on our planet. And one way or another that abuse is rebounding on us. It is little wonder that ' . . . the whole creation has been groaning as in the pains of childbirth right up to the present time' (Romans 8.22).

Fortunately, though, it is not all gloom and doom. There is a growing awareness of environmental problems today which is having some effect. Some farmers are turning to more traditional farming methods and some market gardeners are producing organically grown vegetables and fruit. Vocal environmental groups are bringing about pressure at governmental level and this whole movement is undergirded by the increasing number of people who are concerned about their diet and who are changing to wholefoods.

But how should the Christian respond? Certainly we should not ignore this issue or be discouraged, which is all too easy when we look at the scale of the problem, involving economies, governments and huge multi-national companies. We feel helpless and cannot see how we could possibly change the minds and direction of these political and economic giants. This is what Moses felt when God asked him to lead the Israelites out of Egypt (Exodus 3.11), and Gideon when asked to defeat the Midianites (Judges 6:15). Yet look at what God did through them. We tend to forget that the Creator is our Father and that he is our strength and hope. And our starting point is ourselves. If we take our role as stewards of creation seriously, we can rely on God to show us the changes we can make in our own lifestyles that will benefit us, the environment and the poor. What better place to start than with diet?

How do we find out what God wants? Firstly, by recognising that we are stewards of creation through God and are accountable to him for the way in which we use it. Secondly by asking forgiveness for ways in which we know we have abused our bodies and creation and have neglected the needy. There is also a case for repenting on behalf of the nation. Thirdly, by examining our diet prayerfully and asking God to show us the changes we can make to live healthily and abundantly on less, so that we reduce the amount of waste in our lives, spend money more wisely and live in harmony with the environment. At the same time, we can learn more about the needs of the poor, and other aspects of pollution.

This may take a little time, and there will be failures too, but don't worry; we are called to be faithful, not to succeed, and we can always start again. But as time goes on and we begin to live on less, eating more according to need than to fancy, it will become clearer just how much we have in terms of increased health and energy, spare money and greater awareness of life beyond our own immediate horizon. We will also begin to appreciate how much more there is that we can do.

Further Reading

Hill, Clifford, *The Day Comes*. Fount, 1982.
Moss, Rowland, *The Earth in Our Hands*. IVP, 1982.
Sider, Ronald J., *Rich Christians in an Age of Hunger*. Hodder, 1978.
Taylor John V., *Enough is Enough*. SCM Press, 1975.

Healthy Eating

The health of a nation depends very much on the food it eats. From the abundance of food available today, plus the amount of literature on the role of food in the body, you would think that we were bursting with health and vitality.

But unfortunately we are not. There are still cases of malnutrition in Britain, especially among the elderly, where approximately 3 per cent suffer from chronic and severe malnutrition and a larger percentage suffer from milder forms. There is also a growing awareness that there is malnutrition among some of the ethnic minorities who have not adapted their diet to cope with climatic changes.

The main area of concern in the West, though, is over-nutrition, that is, eating too much of certain types of foods. According to the 1982 Public Expenditure Survey, the average family of four spent £35.84 per week on food, consisting mostly of meat, dairy products such as milk, eggs and cheese, and refined and convenience foods. Nutritionists now recognise that this diet is linked with a whole host of diseases that include heart and bowel disease, diverticulitis, diabetes, obesity, high blood pressure and other health problems which are only found in the western developed countries. It also has an effect on our moral and mental health. In fact, despite the amount of food available today, we are less healthy than during the last war when food was rationed.

Fortunately all this research and literature is having an effect on some sections of the community, and there is a ground swell of interest in healthy eating. It is no longer thought to be eccentric or synonymous with sandals and nut cutlets; sound nutrition has become respectable. We can see that from the recent growth in the number of health food shops, which are springing up in every town, and from the wide variety of people who use them.

Generally, though, the level of awareness of healthy eating is very low and our choice of food seems to be influenced by a number of factors. Sometimes people overeat from boredom, loneliness, anxiety or an attempt to satisfy the body's cravings for nutrients that it is not receiving from its diet. Others overeat out of habit, believing they need three large square meals a day, even though they are older and less active. This is one of the main causes of obesity among the elderly. Often the husband determines the diet in the family, yet usually he knows least about food values. Some fall under the spell of advertising, believing that refined and processed foods are good for them, whilst many look to their doctor for advice on nutrition, not realising that many doctors know very little about it because it is given scant coverage in medical schools. And generally there is very little education in schools, or by the health service, on healthy eating as a way of preventing illness and maintaining health.

Whatever the reason for a poor diet, nutritionists can identify a common problem: these people are all eating refined foods and additives and have too much salt, fat and sugar in their diet, and this is damaging their health.

Salt

The average westerner eats approximately 10 g (about ½ oz) of salt a day, when in fact 200 mg at the most is sufficient in a moderate climate.

It is very hard to avoid salt if you eat a lot of convenience foods. It is added to all shop bought bread, cakes and pastries; it is used to flavour all convenience, tinned and frozen food, and savoury snacks like crisps and nuts are coated with it, as are meats such as bacon and ham. It is also one of the main ingredients in gravy mixes, packeted soups, stock cubes and drinks like Bovril. Then, apart from all that, we add it to the cooking water and season the food again at the table to bring out the flavour! Have you noticed how people automatically reach for the salt shaker before tasting their food to see if it needs extra salt?

Large quantities of salt in the diet are harmful and can lead to serious health problems. It contributes to obesity, which strains the heart and kidneys, and this can lead to high blood pressure and possibly to kidney disease and coronary heart disease which is the single greatest cause of death among men, with women catching up.

Those adults who have given up salt often find that they lose weight and their blood pressure is reduced. They also rediscover the true flavour of food, or make more use of herbs and spices, which add a new and healthy dimension to their diet.

Sugar
Refined white sugar is another commodity hard to avoid in our western diet because it is used in all processed and convenience foods. We find it in jams, cakes, jellies, soft drinks, ice cream, preserves, frozen foods etc. The list is endless and does not include the sweets we eat or the sugar we spoon into our tea and coffee.

The average person in Britain consumes about 95 lbs of sugar a year, which works out at nearly 2 lbs per person a week. This includes children, who develop a sweet tooth from an early age with sweetened syrups etc. and continue this habit through childhood into adulthood with sweets and soft drinks.

Refined sugar contains empty calories only, all the other nutrients having been lost during the refining process. And as sugar suppresses the appetite for more wholesome foods, children who eat a lot of sugary foods are not getting the nutrients they need to grow healthily. This can lead to problems such as obesity, high blood pressure, heart disease, diabetes and dental decay later on in life.

Fat

If we eat large quantities of meat, dairy products and convenience foods we are also eating quite a lot of saturated animal fat. Pork pies contain 27 per cent fat, sausage rolls 36 per cent and cakes 26 per cent. Chips are also fried in it to give them that distinctive flavour that we like so much.

Our bodies do need fat, but in the West we eat much more than we need, and this is where our problems begin. Any surplus fat is stored in the tissues of the body. This can lead to obesity and increased cholesterol levels in the bloodstream, which eventually choke up the walls of the coronary arteries supplying blood to the heart and so can contribute to coronary heart disease. Originally it was mainly old people who suffered from this problem, but now the age range is widening and there are increasing numbers of heart attacks among younger people, including children who are brought up on savoury snacks and chips with everything.

Refined foods

Much of the food we eat today is refined, which means that it lacks fibre. The outer covering of wheat is removed during milling to give flour a smooth fine texture and our rice is polished to remove the husks. Then we continue the refining process in the home by peeling fruit and vegetables and cooking them until they are soft and soggy. Nutritionists now know that a lack of fibre in the diet can cause problems such as constipation, varicose veins, diverticulitis and cancer of the bowel. It is also linked with gallstones, appendicitis, dental decay, heart disease and piles.

Additives

The food industry uses about 3,000 additives in convenience foods. These tend to fall into two categories. There are the fortifying or nutritive additives, designed to replace some of the nutrients lost in the refining process. Some of these additives are of organic origin, but most are synthetic copies of natural chemicals. They could be harmless, but they are not as well absorbed by the body as the natural ones and so do not feed us. It is also known that whilst many nutrients are lost in the refining process, only one or two are replaced by the food manufacturers.

The non-nutritive additives are used to flavour, colour, preserve, emulsify and improve the taste and appearance of food. They are also used to prolong shelf life, upgrade poor quality foods and prevent any deterioration in the foods.

The average person consumes about 10 lb of these additives each year. Of the 3,000 used in the processing of food, 600 synthetic additives are not naturally found in food and so far food manufacturers monitor only 300 of the entire number for their effects on health. This means that research into food additives has a long way to go. We know that many additives accumulate in the body, but we do not know what their long term effect is on our health. Nor do we know how compound chemicals, such as the two or three hundred chemicals needed to make coffee flavouring for cakes and sweets, interact with each other, or the effect they have on the body.

The other problem is that there are no standard international laws governing additives in food. Regulations vary considerably from country to country. Coal tar food dyes, for instance, are banned in Britain because of their link with allergies, cancer and mental disturbances, but they are still used in the United States and could unwittingly be eaten by the British in imported foods.

Nor can you ever be certain of the safety of an additive. Cyclamate, an artificial sweetner, was considered safe for years until further research showed otherwise and it was banned. Some additives are still being used which are suspected of being harmful. Monosodium glutamate (MSG) is one. This is widely used in commercial foods to bring out the flavour but it is suspected of causing liver damage and allergic reactions and it is known to cause the 'Chinese restaurant syndrome' – a dizzy feeling experienced by some people after a Chinese meal. Other additives like nitrates and nitrites, are considered by some researchers to be pure poison, yet they have been used for years to cure meats like bacon and ham.

Independent research on additives, carried out by Great Ormond Street hospital and others, links them increasingly with allergies, certain types of cancer, poor learning abilities and behavioural disturbances in children and adults. Studies carried out by Alec Schauss, Director of the American Institute for Biosocial Research in Washington, among aggressive prison inmates in three different American states, showed that behaviour returned to normal quite quickly when they were given a wholefood diet free from additives and low in salt, sugar and fat.

If you wish to know what additives are added to your food, check the list of ingredients on the packet. Additives are referred to either by name or by an E number and are listed in order of quantity, with the highest at the top. You can find out more about them and their effects on health by referring to the book recommended in the Further Reading section at the end of this chapter.

This situation poses questions that we need to answer, as Christians who should be concerned to avoid poor eating habits. Firstly, can we justify processing all the nutrients out of wholesome food and replacing them with additives, which, although they might not harm us, will certainly not feed us? Is this not an abuse of the food and our bodies? Not only that, but these convenience foods are expensive, so we are paying more for less. The expense does not end there. Life insurance premiums rise as our life expectancy is reduced. Then there is the waste of resources in paper for packaging and medicines for treatment. And lastly, but most important, how are we glorifying God by being sick and overweight when it could be avoided? Would it not be more obedient, cheaper and healthier to eat foods that we know will feed us?

A car is designed to run on petrol and it will not move an inch if you put anything else in the tank. Even then the car will perform differently according to the grade of petrol used. The human body needs certain foods to function properly and this is why we eat – to provide the fuel the body needs to stay healthy and vital. If some necessary nutrients are missing, or of a poor quality, the body will eventually build up disease, malfunction and break down.

So what should we eat to stay healthy? According to the James Report produced by NACNE (National Advisory Committee on Nutrition Education), we should eat a fresh wholefood diet with plenty of fibre, which means wholewheat breads and pastries, unpolished rice and plenty of fresh fruit and vegetables. They recommend that we eat less meat, especially the fatty kinds such as pork and mutton, and make more use of fish, pulses and unpolished rice. They recommend that we eat a moderate amount of dairy products but drastically reduce our intake of sugar, salt and fat, making more use of vegetable oils rather than animal fat. Refined and convenience foods should be kept to a minimum. If we eat foods as near as possible to their natural state, that is, unrefined, raw or lightly cooked, the body will get all the nutrients it needs to stay healthy. These necessary nutrients fall into six main categories: proteins, carbohydrates, fats, vitamins, minerals and trace elements, and water.

Proteins
These are found in all the cells of the body. They are complex chemicals that are vital for growth, helping to make up the structure of skin, muscle, bones, teeth and blood. There are thousands of different proteins in the body and each has its specific role to build, fight infection and to regulate the biochemical functions of the body.

All these proteins are formed from combinations of twenty amino acids. Eight essential amino acids must be supplied by the diet so that the body can make the rest, and as meat, fish, poultry and dairy products such as eggs, milk, cheese and yoghurt contain all eight essential amino acids, they form our chief source of protein.

Plant proteins such as cereals (wheat and rye), grains (rice) and pulses (beans and lentils) are rich sources of proteins too, but lack one or more of the essential amino acids and are incomplete proteins. However, if they are eaten in combination with each other – like, for instance, beans on toast, macaroni cheese or rice pudding (rice and milk) – all the essential amino acids are present and they become a source of complete protein.

From the recent famine pictures we have a very clear idea of what protein deficiency can do. There is a wasting of muscles, premature ageing, poor growth in children, retarded mental development, fatigue, anaemia and increased susceptibility to infection. Generally this is not a problem in the western world. On average we over-eat protein by about 50 per cent. But this does not make us any healthier as any excess protein is broken down and stored to be used as energy later. This makes protein an expensive energy source.

Carbohydrates
In Third World countries carbohydrates, or starch, form up to 90 per cent of the diet, compared with 40 per cent in the West. The body needs carbohydrate for a variety of reasons: for proper brain function, to maintain body temperature and to supply energy. In fact, any bodily movement, from raising an eyebrow to an arm, takes energy and this is supplied by carbohydrate and fat.

There are three main sources of carbohydrate: sugar, starch and fibre. Until 150 years ago our energy was supplied mainly by starchy foods like bread, cereals, rice, potatoes and pulses. Then sugar was introduced and refined sugar, together with refined flour, is now our largest source of carbohydrate.

As has been said, all nutrients have been removed from refined white sugar so that, unlike starch, it consists only of calories. Yet refined sugar suppresses the desire for wholesome and nutritious food and this is a contributory factor in many western diseases.

Nutritionists now realise that fibre is an important part of our diet and is instrumental in keeping us healthy. It attracts harmful bacteria and toxic substances such as artificial colouring and flavouring and sweeps them from the bowel like a broom. It adds bulk to food by swelling with water in the colon and this makes us feel full and more satisfied with less. For this reason it is a valuable slimming aid, but it would be unwise to eat huge amounts of bran because that would be as harmful as eating none at all. The digestive tract was designed to process food quickly, but foods in our western diet may lie in the intestine for days. Fibre transports food through the tract more quickly and regulates the absorption of sugars and fats by the bloodstream, keeping energy supplies constant and helping to prevent the mid-morning 'flag' which is due to low blood sugar levels. A newly discovered soluble fibre, found mainly in oats, also helps to reduce the levels of sugar and cholesterol in the blood and so lowers the risk of heart disease.

Fats
These are made from chemical building blocks called fatty acids. There are forty altogether and we need three essential fatty acids from our diet to make up the rest.

The two sources of fat are: saturated animal fat from meat, dairy products and lard, and polyunsaturated fats from fish and from plant oils such as sunflower oil, safflower oil and others.

Fats are necessary to carry fat-soluble vitamins A, D, E and K around the body to maintain a healthy skin, healthy teeth and eyesight and to provide resistance to infection.

Fat also provides a very compact source of energy: one gram of fat will provide nine calories compared with four calories per gram from carbohydrates. It slows down the emptying time of the stomach and contributes to that feeling of fulness and satisfaction at the end of a meal. This is why fried foods are so popular. It also adds to the taste and texture of foods. Fat is necessary to form a protective layer around vital organs like the heart and kidneys and under the skin to protect our nerves and reduce the effect of the cold on the body.

Fat deficiency leads to skin disorders, lethargy, poor hair, poor skin, muscles, bones and teeth, as well as causing hunger pangs between meals. Fat deficiency is rarely a problem in the West, though; rather, the reverse is true and all nutritionists agree that we should reduce our fat intake generally to about 1–2 ozs (25–50 g) a day and make greater use of cold-pressed vegetable oils and soft margarines.

Vitamins
These are chemicals needed by the body in small amounts to help the body carry out its biochemical processes properly; processes such as converting fat and carbohydrates into energy and repairing damaged tissues. Each vitamin has its specific role, but they work in combination and so a deficiency in one may well affect the working of them all.

New vitamins are being discovered and named, but as yet we do not know their function. The thirteen that we do know about fall into two groups. These are the fat-soluble vitamins A, D, E, K which occur in fatty foods such as meat, milk, butter, fish and eggs and are needed for healthy skin, hair, eyesight and vitality. These are stored in the tissues and used as required. The other group, the B complex and Vitamin C are water-soluble and are needed to fight infection, to protect the nerves and help bodily growth. These vitamins cannot be stored; the body takes what it needs and the surplus is lost through sweat and urine.

Vitamin deficiencies lead to illness and disease. A lack of

vitamin A found in liver, eggs and carrots, leads to skin problems and night blindess, whilst a lack of vitamin B$_{12}$ makes us nervous and jumpy. It is important to get an adequate supply of vitamins from our diet.

Minerals and trace elements
These are inorganic chemicals needed by the body to regulate metabolic processes. For example, they maintain the water balance in the body, help glands to work properly and affect muscle response. They also help in the building of bones, teeth and soft tissue like muscle and nervous tissues.

The main minerals, which are used in larger quantities by the body, are iron, calcium, iodine, magnesium, phosphorus, chloride, potassium and sodium. If we eat plenty of fresh fruit and vegetables with a wholefood diet, we should get all the minerals and trace elements the body needs to function properly. We should ensure particularly that we have adequate amounts of calcium to prevent among other things rickets (a malformation of the bones which was common earlier in this century and now common among some ethnic minorities), and iron to prevent anaemia which is especially common among pregnant and menstruating women.

As well as the main minerals already described, many others are found in minute quantities in the body, hence their name 'trace elements'. These include copper, chromium and zinc and it is not certain as yet what role these minerals play in the body.

Supplements
The use of vitamin supplements is a highly contentious area among scientists today. Some believe that our modern diet is so adulterated that we need vitamins to compensate for the lost nutrients. And there are some in this category, like Paulus Lining, who are using very large doses of vitamins

to cure diseases such as arthritis, with some success. There are others, though, who are uncertain of the effects of large doses of synthetic vitamins and believe we should make sure we get all the vitamins and minerals we need from a balanced diet.

This is something we should learn more about so that we can make up our own minds. Personally, I fall midway between the two arguments. I would steer clear of megadoses and would only use them on medical advice and under medical supervision. And I do agree that we should get our nutrients from our food. But there are occasions when vitamin and mineral supplements are useful. If we have been ill or undernourished from years of wrong eating, then our food could do with a little help as it builds us up again. So a course of natural vitamins such as brewer's yeast tablets for the B vitamin complex, cod liver oil for vitamins A, D, E and K and calcium tablets, taken in moderation, add a valuable boost to the diet until we reach a point where the diet can take over and be solely responsible for feeding the body.

Now, before I eulogise about a sound and healthy diet, I do want to say that I do not believe that nutrition is the universal cure for all the world's diseases and ills. They would not all disappear if everyone suddenly adopted a healthy diet. There are other factors which affect health, such as lack of sleep and exercise, stress, our spiritual state and sin itself. Jesus is the only answer to all our problems. But I do believe that healthy eating can do away with many of the problems that we have learnt to live with – colds and coughs, fatigue, emotional and behavioural problems, poor posture, digestive problems and allergies – plus those we have already considered earlier on in this chapter. Elderly people suffer from many of these and they have become so commonplace that we now think that illness is a natural outcome of age, and that to die of an illness is natural. I do not agree with this and though we do slow down with age, I think that God designed our bodies to function properly until the end of our lives, and they would do so if only we would take care of them.

There are many encouraging stories of people becoming more healthy and alert once they have changed to wholefoods. Nagging problems they have had for years have disappeared, depression often lifts and fatigue ebbs away. They are also less susceptible to colds and other infections, which results in fewer visits to the doctor. Other people have recovered completely from crippling diseases like arthritis and asthma when under medically supervised diets, while many drug addicts, alcoholics and smokers have found it much easier to give up their dependencies when fed wholefoods high in B vitamins.

It was a great help to me too and instrumental in my conversion. A few years ago I was not in the best of health. I was prey to any prevailing infection, constantly exhausted and invariably depressed and withdrawn. My hair was stringy and hung like limp rats' tails and my skin had the quality of Aertex. Life was a real burden.

I knew that much of this had to do with my lifestyle and diet which had nothing to recommend them. I would breakfast on coffee and a cigarette if there was time, and dash to school. By breaktime I would virtually crawl to the staff room for a cigarette and coffee booster to see me through to the school lunch, which, despite good intentions, was usually overcooked and stodgy. There were tea and flapjacks at four and anything that came to hand for the evening meal. I would be out most evenings until the early hours, smoking and drinking quite heavily, and usually woke up with a hangover.

The odd emotional crisis did not help, and when I contracted amoebic dysentery for the third time in four months (I was living in Kenya at the time) I knew I had to do something about this, but did not know what. At that point someone gave me a book on nutrition and within a week I was a different person. The lethargy vanished and I became more vital. Gradually I became more outgoing, my skin and hair improved, so did my temper and the constant visits to the doctor for antibiotics stopped.

I gave up cigarettes and spirits, too, because I found them distasteful and began to have more energy and vision to put my life in order. I did more of the things I really wanted to do, rather than following the herd as I had done before.

Within a few months I had life the way I had always wanted it. I gave up the constant parties and discos and spent more time with good friends or in the bush, walking and watching the animals. Yet the odd thing is that I soon realised that I was not happy. There was something missing and it was not until someone casually mentioned the word 'God' in conversation that I knew what it was and became a Christian some months later.

It is amazing the methods that God uses to bring us to him. I believe that he initiated that change of diet, knowing that it would take my mind off my physical and emotional state and raise me up so that I could peer over the rim of my despair and see the way to him.

What sound nutrition has done for some it can do for us all. Constant visits to the doctor with problems that can be avoided by healthy eating do not glorify God in any way, and that is what we are here for. It is true that he can use illness for his own purposes and there are some people specifically called to a very simple diet, but generally a poor diet is an abuse of our bodies which are God's gift to us. Healthy eating is an important part of our stewardship and our witness. It also gives us the peace of mind that comes from knowing that we are using our bodies and God's resources properly.

Those with serious food-related problems should find it helpful to consult a registered nutritionist who will provide a specialised diet. But those with no serious problem who want to get the most out of their food and lives can learn more by further reading or by taking various courses on nutrition.

It will take a little time to sort out and change to the

correct types of food, but the rewards are worth it and once we are more familiar with it, healthy eating need not dominate our thoughts and time, it can just become a natural part of our lives.

Further Reading

Bingham, S. *Nutrition: Better Health Through Good Eating*. Corgi 1978.
Burkitt, D., *Don't Forget Fibre in Your Diet*. Martin Dunitz 1980.
Davis, A. *Let's Stay Healthy*. Unwin Paperbacks 1982.
Hanssen, M., *'E' For Additives*. Thorsons, 1984.
Loewenfeld, C., *Everything You Should Know About Your Food*. Faber 1978.
Sider, Ronald J., *Living More Simply*. Hodder 1980.

Useful Organisations

McCarrison Society 23 Stanley Court, Worcester Road, Sutton, Surrey SM2 6SD. Gives advice on general nutrition and can make referrals to other societies and organisations.
Coronary Prevention Group, ARMS/CPG Unit, Central Middlesex Hospital, Acton Lane, London NW10 7NF. Give advice on prevention of heart attacks that includes nutrition, diet, high blood pressure and smoking.

Protein Foods

In this chapter we will have a look at the different sources of protein, both animal – meat, fish, poultry and dairy products – and the vegetarian alternatives – nuts and pulses.

Meat
Meat from any domesticated animal, whether cow, pig, or sheep, is a valuable source of protein, iron, phosphorus, sulphur and the B group of vitamins. The most tender and leanest cuts of meat are: fillet steak, thick flank, rump steak and sirloin, from beef; chops, tenderloin and ham, from pork; and chops, leg and best end of neck from mutton. These also tend to be the most expensive cuts of meat. But this does not mean that they are the most nutritious. Muscle meats have less protein and other nutrients than organ meats like liver, kidneys and sweetbreads, which contain a whole range of nutrients and are especially high in vitamins A, B and D. They have less fat and can be bought at a fraction of the cost of the more expensive cuts. Cheaper and tougher cuts of meat, such as brisket, oxtail and neck of lamb, are also nutritious if cooked slowly on a gentle heat with as much fat as possible removed before and after cooking.

Try to reduce the amount of meat you eat to help cut down your fat intake. Eat it, say, every other day and introduce your family to the meat alternatives, pulses and nuts. On your meat days try to make more use of the organ meats, leaving expensive joints for special occasions. Whenever possible, avoid chops because although they are very convenient to cook, this benefit is outweighed by the wasted bone and fat which you pay for but do not eat.

Buy your meat from a butcher rather than the supermarket. Get to know him, and learn more about cuts of meat. When selecting your meat, make sure it is fresh by examining the flesh and the fat. The flesh of muscle meats should be firm, fine-grained and slightly elastic and the fat should be white or creamy-yellow and free from any discoloration.

Very often butchers use a red dye to freshen up jaded meats and make them look appetising. Find out if your butcher dyes his meat and if he does, change to one who does not.

Sausages contain large amounts of rusk and chemicals nowadays, so avoid them unless you have found a good local butcher who makes his own. Minced beef has a lot of added fat, so select a piece of lean meat and ask your butcher to mince it for you.

If you want to store your meat in the fridge, remove it from the wrapping, place it on a plate and cover with plastic film, leaving both ends open for ventilation. It will keep for two to three days like this. Do exactly the same when thawing frozen meat and let it defrost completely in the fridge before cooking. Do not hasten the defrosting process by pouring boiling water over it. This kills off some of the nutrients.

Cool cooked meat completely before freezing it, and thaw it out again thoroughly when you want to use it. Recook meat thoroughly, for at least ten minutes, to kill off any possible harmful bacteria. Cooked meat can be stored in the fridge for a day or two, wrapped in plastic film to stop the meat drying out and curling up at the edges.

Offal and minced meat are particularly perishable, so keep them in the fridge and use within twenty-four hours. They will keep longer in the freezer.

Just before cooking meat, remove all visible fat and cook slowly on a gentle heat to prevent shrinkage and loss of nutrients. Casseroles and stews are particularly nutritious, and dishes cooked in a slow cooker too, because the nutrients in slowly cooked food are retained by the juices. If you are roasting meat, use a roasting bag to reduce the nutrient loss, or a Romertopf, an open-pored earthenware casserole dish with a tightly fitting lid, that cooks the meat in its own juices and prevents shrinkage.

Poultry
Chicken contains the same nutrients as red meat, but has less fat, which makes it a valuable meat for slimmers and those suffering from heart disease. Try, whenever possible, to buy free-range chickens, as most of the cheaper ones sold in supermarkets have been battery-reared and treated with antibiotics, sedatives and hormones which can be passed on to the consumer. The skin has also been bleached white to make it more appealing to the customer.

Store and cook chicken in the same way as red meat and always remember to thaw the bird thoroughly in the refrigerator before cooking. And do not forget to remove the giblets in their plastic bag before you put the bird in the oven!

Turkey is another useful bird which is now becoming less expensive and widely available throughout the year instead of just at Christmas. Store, cook and use it as you would chicken. Ducks and geese tend to be very fatty, so save them for special occasions.

Fish
Fish is an excellent source of protein, calcium, iodine and vitamins A, B, D and E. The fat is also unsaturated, so even the oiliest fish, like mackerel, are safe to eat because there is no build-up of cholesterol in the bloodstream.

Due to over-fishing and sea pollution, fish is not as plentiful as it was, but try to include it as a regular part of the diet and vary the fish regularly to avoid a build-up of toxins in the body from polluted fishing areas.

Buy fish from a fishmonger and get to know him. Make sure that the flesh of the fish is plump and firm and the eyes clear. Mackerel, herring, whiting, coley and sprats are nutritious and inexpensive types of fish, and the more expensive ones such as cod, plaice, halibut and sole can be flaked and mixed with rice or other foods to make them go further.

Avoid packeted or smoked fish. They are expensive and usually have been treated with food dyes which could be harmful.

As fish deteriorates very quickly, eat it within twenty-four hours. It will keep longer if frozen, but make sure that the fish has not been frozen before, otherwise a second freezing will detexturise it and the flesh will become pulpy and unpalatable.

Buy fish whole and clean it at home. Use the heads and tails to make a fish stock which can be frozen and used in other fish dishes.

Try not to boil the fish when cooking, as up to half the nutrients will be lost in the cooking water. Instead, bake, fry or grill fish very gently and briefly until the flesh turns white. It will keep its shape and most of its nutrients this way.

Shellfish is another valuable protein source and your fishmonger can advise on the selection and cooking of crabs, lobsters and prawns. If you decide to collect your own winkles, mussels and cockles from the seashore, choose an unpolluted area and keep the shellfish alive for a day or two in a bucket of fresh water. Change the water every six to seven hours to filter the shellfish clean. Then place the shellfish in a pan of cold water, bring it to the boil slowly and simmer for ten to fifteen minutes.

Remove the beard from mussels, and discard any that are open before cooking and any that are closed after cooking.

Cooking shellfish is always an emotional occasion for me because the thought of plunging live creatures into boiling water makes me feel faint. Instead, I place the live shellfish in a pan of cold water and heat it slowly in the belief that they pass out as the water heats up and are unconscious by the time it gets too hot for comfort.

Eggs

Eggs are a quick and convenient source of nourishment and are always useful to have in the house. They contain protein, vitamin A, and riboflavin from the B group of vitamins, plus iron and calcium. They also contain fat in a concentrated form and so nutritionists recommend that we restrict the number of eggs we eat to between three and five a week, excluding the eggs used as ingredients in other dishes.

Most of the eggs we buy today in supermarkets come from battery farms and tend to have thin pale shells, less flavour and less nutritional value as well. Buy free range eggs, or deep litter eggs if you can. They are becoming increasingly available now as demand grows.

Eggs will keep well in the fridge, but keep some at room temperature as they cook better this way. Try to use them up within a week or two. Although they do not lose their nutrients, they tend to lose their flavour and become rather leathery when cooked if they are kept too long.

Milk

Milk is one of those versatile protein foods which can be used in sweet and savoury dishes or turned into other foods such as cheese and yoghurt. These are just as nourishing as milk and add variety to the menu.

Milk has a reasonably high protein content and is a valuable protein source for vegetarians. It also contains calcium, phosphorus and small amounts of vitamins A, B, C, D and E, as well as easily digested fats and carbohydrates and minerals. It does not contain iron, though, which we need for the formation of blood, and so it should be given to children with wholegrain cereals, or another iron rich food.

There are other types of milk available from healthfood shops today, such as goat's milk, and even soya milk made from soya beans. These tend to be more expensive than cow's milk, but some people find that they suit them better, particularly soya bean milk which is easily digested by those who are allergic to ordinary milk.

Raw milk, straight from the cow, is sold in only a very few areas. Most milk has been heated in some way to destroy harmful bacteria. The least destructive method used is pasteurisation which sterilises the milk at a low temperature, so that most of the nutrients are retained. UHT milk has been heated to an ultra-high temperature, and though the protein content is intact, most of the vitamins have been lost.

Skimmed milk is ideal for slimmers because most of the fat content has been removed, but then so have the fat-soluble vitamins A and D. The same can be said of dried milk which has also lost most of the B and C vitamins during the drying process. Because of this, nutritionists recommend that it is *not* given to babies or growing children in place of ordinary milk.

Heat and light reduce the nutrients in milk, so take your pint off the doorstep as soon as possible if you have it delivered, and store it in the fridge, or a cool dark place, where it will stay fresh for a couple of days. Keep milk covered to prevent it absorbing flavours from other foods.

Yoghurt is milk clotted by a lactic bacterium and is an inexpensive and nourishing food. It is especially useful to slimmers because the milk sugar has been used up by the bacteria in the clotting process.

It also helps to keep the body working healthily in a variety of ways. It reduces infection by preventing the growth of harmful bacteria in the intestines, it speeds up the rate of digestion, relieves indigestion and keeps healthy intestinal bacteria flourishing.

Make your own yoghurt at home if you can; it is easy and much cheaper than the commercial brands, and free from additives (see recipe on p. 151). It will keep well in the fridge for a few days, but do not keep it too long because the bacteria are still working and will produce more acid, giving the yoghurt a sharp flavour. There is not much chance of that happening, though – home-made yoghurt will become so popular that you will have difficulty in keeping up with demand.

Cheese is a great addition to many dishes and is highly nutritious, containing protein, vitamin A, fat, phosphorus and calcium. The hard cheeses tend to be one third protein, one third fat and one third water, and though it is a valuable protein source for vegetarians, the rest of us should use it carefully, making sure that it is well balanced with other nutrients and does not overload the body with additional calories.

Hard cheeses like English and Irish Cheddar are strongly flavoured and ideal for cooking. The milder ones are better eaten in salads or sandwiches. All hard cheeses will keep in the fridge for some time if they are well wrapped.

If you find hard cheese difficult to digest, grate it, to make it lighter on the stomach.

Foreign holidays and entry into the Common Market have broadened the range of cheeses available in this country. There are the soft French cheeses like Brie and Camembert which are ideal for the after dinner cheese board. They are best kept at room temperature, and Camembert especially should be kept until it has a ripe smell and a runny centre. Then there are the Italian cheeses, Mozzarella, Ricotta and Parmesan, which give Italian dishes their distinctive flavour, plus many more to choose from in your local delicatessen, where you can buy the quantities that you need. Ask for a sliver to taste when making your selection and avoid those which contain additives.

Cream and cottage cheese are made from fermented milk solids separated from the whey.

Cream cheese is easy to make at home (see recipe on p. 151) and, like yoghurt, is cheaper and free from additives found in commercial brands.

It will keep in the fridge indefinitely, but use cream cheese sparingly as it has a high fat content, and make more use of cottage cheese which has had most of the fat removed.

Nuts

Nuts are very popular with vegetarians because they are a highly nutritious and concentrated meat alternative. Three-quarters of an ounce of nuts is equivalent to an ounce of meat or fish. They are rich in protein, fibre, starch and vitamins B and E, plus phosphorus and potassium. With the exception of cashew and coconuts, which contain saturated fats, most nuts contain unsaturated fats. So, although they are fattening and an adult should eat them carefully, there will be no build-up of cholesterol in the bloodstream.

There is quite a selection to choose from: almonds, walnuts, hazelnuts, brazil nuts, peanuts and sunflower seeds. Buy them loose and unsalted and store in an airtight container in a cool, dark place until you use them, to prevent the fat turning rancid. If possible, buy them in their shells and remove just before using them, as this way they keep fresher longer.

Use them in nut roasts and nut cutlets as a meat substitute, combine them with rice (see recipe for Peanut Paella, p. 128) and add them to desserts, fruit salads, cakes or the breakfast muesli. Eat them with raisins as a snack between meals, or convert them into a nut-cream and mix with fruit juice or milk. Almonds are especially suitable for this purpose.

Pulses

Pulses are dried peas, beans and lentils and belong to the leguminosae family, from which we get the word 'legumes', a name given to any vegetable that comes in a pod. There are about 14,000 varieties of legumes grown throughout the world today, and for centuries they have been the staple food of eastern countries. The Israelites used them too: Esau sold his birthright for a pottage of lentils (Genesis 25.30–4) and David was brought lentils and beans when he went to Mahanaim to escape from Absalom (2 Samuel 17.28).

Until recent years beans have not been very popular in Britain. One or two varieties were familiar, such as red lentils, dried peas and butter beans, but apart from that, beans remained a foreign food. That situation seems to be changing now. The rising cost of meat and concern for health has led many to experiment with pulses as a meat substitute, with the result that a colourful selection of beans in all shapes and sizes is now on sale in healthfood and Indian food shops.

As beans are a plant protein they need to be eaten in combination with each other, or with another plant protein such as wheat or rice, to become a complete protein. They are high in protein, fibre, calcium, iron, riboflavine and nicotinic acid from the B group of vitamins. They are low in fat and high in carbohydrates, which makes them an ideal energy food. They also have the bonus of being a fraction of the cost of meat, yet are just as nutritious if care is taken in preparation and blending of foods.

Like nuts, they are very versatile. You can use them in soups, casseroles, rissoles, stews, loaves and salads. You can sprout the smaller pulses, such as adzuki and mung beans to use stir-fried or in salads (see recipe section for method) or you can buy tofu, a bean curd made from soya flour, to use in the same way as cottage cheese.

Buy beans loose from healthfood shops or Indian food shops – they are cheaper that way; and buy in small quantities, unless you intend to use a lot of them. Although they are dried, if kept too long, say longer than a year, they will become so hard that no amount of soaking will soften them. Soya bean is the most nutritious pulse; it has twice the protein content of the other beans. Chick peas, black-eyed beans and lentils have delicious flavours and are my favourites, but it is worth experimenting with them yourself to see which ones you and your family like best.

Rinse all beans thoroughly in cold water before cooking to clean them, and remove any stones or twigs. Soak the harder beans overnight in a covered bowl to reduce the cooking time. Red lentils or split peas do not need to be soaked; they only take about twenty minutes to cook. They do need to be rinsed thoroughly before cooking, though.

Save time and money by cooking batches of beans in the pressure cooker, if you have one, and freeze what you do not need immediately. If you do not have a pressure cooker, bring the beans to the boil in a covered saucepan, turn down the heat and simmer gently until they are soft but crisp.

When using more than one type of bean, cook them together, if they have the same cooking time, but separately otherwise. Cook red beans, such as adzuki and red kidney beans, separately too, otherwise all the beans will end up a delicate shade of pink.

If the recipe calls for salt, vinegar, tomatoes or lemon juice, add them after the beans have cooked, otherwise they will become tough and indigestible.

And finally, whenever you cook red kidney beans, always boil them rapidly for ten minutes before simmering, to destroy the toxins in the beans.

4

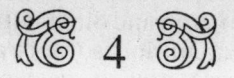

Energy Foods

When Jesus fed the 4,000 on loaves of bread as well as fish (Matthew 15.29–39), he was giving them a balanced meal, because bread, along with other starchy foods such as pastry, pasta and rice, is a carbohydrate and a valuable source of energy. The people needed the energy to walk home after three days without food.

In the western world carbohydrates supply over a third of our energy requirements and are an important part of a balanced diet. But in some poorer countries, carbohydrates make up the bulk of the diet, between 60 and 90 per cent in some cases. This is because starch is usually the cheapest and bulkiest food available, so it satisfies the appetite to some extent and keeps the person alive, but it is not able to keep him alert and healthy.

Every country has its own particular staple foods. Parts of Africa use millet; other parts, such as Kenya, use maize or corn meal; China and Far Eastern countries use rice; whilst we in Britain prefer potatoes and bread, usually made from wheat flour. Now, though, due to the mingling of cultures and a growing interest in foreign foods, new and unfamiliar carbohydrates are appearing in the shops and we have a broader selection to choose from.

Wheat
Most of our bread is made from a hard wheat flour rich in gluten that helps the bread to rise. It is a wholesome grain containing protein, fibre, wheatgerm, some of the vitamin

B complex, calcium, iron and other nutrients in tiny quantities, as well as starch, and so it is an important food, especially for the vegetarian and vegan.

There are several types of wheat flour:

White flour, preferred by commercial food manufacturers and bakers because it has a light texture and a long shelf life. This flour has little food value, as all the nutrients have been bleached and refined out of it. Some synthetic vitamins are added to restore a little food value, but it is incomplete and of a poor quality.

100 per cent wholewheat flour. This is a healthier buy and easily available in supermarkets and health food shops. All its nutrients, i.e. bran, wheatgerm, vitamins and minerals, are intact. It makes a slightly heavier bread than white flour, but is very nourishing, with a delicious nutty flavour, and leaves you satisfied with less. You can buy both plain and self-raising wholewheat flour.

Wholemeal flour. This is slightly lighter than wholewheat flour because it has been partially refined and has lost between 15 and 19 per cent of its bran and wheatgerm. Despite that, it is still more nutritious than white flour.

Try to make your own bread, if possible. It is quite easy and there is little more satisfying than the taste of homemade bread – especially if you have made it yourself! Failing that, buy uncut loaves from the baker. If you *must* buy wrapped bread from the supermarket, check the label to make sure that you are buying wholemeal or wholewheat bread and not white bread dyed brown with caramel colouring.

The wheat grain itself is sold in a variety of forms in healthfood shops:

Kibbled wheat – wholewheat grain cracked between rollers to help it to cook more quickly. It should be boiled for about twenty minutes.

Bulgar or burghul wheat – hulled wheat grain that has been steamed and roasted. This needs little, if any, cooking.

Wheat flakes – wholegrain wheat that has been rolled flatter than kibbled wheat.

These can all be used in breakfast cereals, or to thicken stews and casseroles.

Rye
Rye flour is used to make rye bread, a favourite in Germany and northern Europe. Unrefined rye flour has a dark colour and a tangy flavour and produces a denser loaf than wheat flour because it contains less gluten.

Corn or Maize
We eat it on the cob, as a vegetable, as popcorn at the cinema or to thicken puddings and stews with the finely ground white cornflour starch. Yet it is a staple food in parts of Africa and the USA where it is coarsely ground and used in baking or to make a kind of porridge and also in parts of Europe, such as Southern Italy, where it is known as *polenta*. It has a golden colour and a light, sweet flavour.

Barley
The grain is usually sold as pearl or pot barley and is used to make barley water for drinking and for brewing beer. It is also used to thicken soups or casseroles.

Millet
This can be used as a substitute for rice and is cooked in exactly the same way. It has a fluffy texture and cooks quickly. It can be used in risottos and pilaus and goes well with vegetable dishes.

Oats
Once the regional staple of Scotland, oats have now become the established breakfast cereal for most of the British Isles. They are usually rolled and form the basis of muesli, or are added to milk and water to make porridge. They cook very quickly, in between three to five minutes, and can also be used to thicken stews or soups and to make cakes, biscuits and pancakes.

Rice
This comes in a variety of types: long, short, white or brown.

White rice is more familiar to us than any other variety. It originally came from Patna in India, but is now grown mostly in the USA or Thailand. White rice is refined, having been polished to remove the husk, germ and bran, leaving mainly starch. For this reason it has a very low nutritional value.

Brown rice, on the other hand, both the long grain from India, and the short grain, popular in parts of China and Japan, is unpolished and still retains its bran and germ. Only the inedible husk has been removed. Brown rice has a delicious nutty flavour. It takes about ten minutes longer to cook than white rice.

Rice is a versatile food and can be used as a substitute for bread, potatoes and pasta. It goes well with savoury dishes such as curries and can be used as the basis of a salad, or in puddings. Long grain rice is usually best for savoury dishes and the short grain is suited to risottos or sweet puddings.

All the grains discussed above can be bought whole, flaked or floured and can be used in cereals, to thicken stews and casseroles or can be added to baking to give a variety of taste and texture. Use between 1 and 2 oz (25–50 g) for each 7 oz (200 g) wheat flour.

When buying your grains make sure that they are fresh by buying them in the quantities you need from a health food shop with a quick turnover.

The whole or flaked grains will keep well in a glass or pottery container stored in a cool, dark place. Store wholewheat flour in an airtight container in a cool, dry place and buy quantities that will last a month or two. The fat in the wheatgerm will go rancid if kept too long.

Cooked rice can be stored in the freezer for up to six months and will keep in the fridge for up to a week.

Soya Flour
This is not a grain, but is made from powdered soya bean.

It is full of protein, vitamins and fat, but has no gluten and so cannot be used as a baking flour on its own as it has no raising or binding qualities. It can be added to other flour, though, to boost the nutritional content, in quantities of 1 oz (25 g) soya flour to 7 oz (200 g) wheat flour. It can also be used as a thickening agent for soups and stews.

Buy soya flour in small quantities, about 1 lb (450 g) at a time, and store it as you would the other flours.

Wheatgerm
This is the germ usually removed from the wheat grain during the refining process to produce white flour. It is rich in complete protein, vitamin E and iron, and can be added to flour when baking, in quantities of 1 oz (25 g) to each 8 oz (225 g) to increase the food value. You can also use it in place of breadcrumbs, or add it to muesli or to crumbles and toppings.

Pasta
This came originally from Italy and takes many forms: spaghetti, macaroni, lasagne and many others which are familiar to us today. It is made from durum wheat and water, and also with egg in some varieties, and can be bought fresh or dried, white or wholewheat. White pasta is little more than starch, so buy wholewheat pasta if you can get it. It has more flavour than white pasta and retains most of its nutrients.

Use pasta as a starter to a meal, in place of bread or potatoes, or to give body to stews and casseroles. Where it really excels, though, is in the Italian dishes it was originally designed for. One of the simplest but nicest ways of eating pasta, I find, is to coat cooked spaghetti or noodles with butter and sprinkle with grated Parmesan cheese and perhaps a pinch of freshly chopped basil. It is delicious and makes an inexpensive starter.

Fibre

Until twenty years ago fibre was discarded during the milling and cooking of food because it was considered an impurity. But since Dr Denis Burkitt's discovery that an unrefined diet prevents most of the destructive western food-related diseases, nutritionists now realise that fibre is an important source of carbohydrate and plays a vital role in keeping us healthy (see Chapter 2).

There are two main sources of fibre. Bran is the hard outer covering of grains such as wheat; this is always removed during the milling of white flour, but is retained in wholewheat flour. The other source is the softer fibre from the skins and skeletons of fruit and vegetables. Both are vital to the digestive system.

Most of the fibre passes unchanged through the digestive tract, but soluble fibre, found mainly in oats, is absorbed into the bloodstream and helps to reduce the risk of heart disease.

Sugar

Sugar occurs naturally in fruit and some vegetables as fructose, and in milk as lactose, but the sugar we normally use is sucrose, which is the refined sugar of sugar beet or sugar cane, and this is not found naturally.

Within the last 150 years sugar has become the dominant source of food energy in the West, and refined white sugar, which has no other nutrients but calories, is widely used in commercial foods and drinks. This is one of the main causes of heart disease, obesity and tooth decay.

If you eat a balanced diet and each meal contains food from the major food groups – protein, fat, carbohydrates, vitamins and minerals – there will be little need for extra sugar and the meal will help to satisfy any cravings for sweet foods. But when extra sugar is necessary use another, less refined sugar source, that contains other nutrients as well.

Molasses and raw cane sugar are made from partially refined sugar cane and contain small quantities of B vitamins, iron and copper. Health food shops stock the widest range of sugars and you can buy it loose in the quantities you need. If you buy your sugar from supermarkets or general grocery shops, check the label to make sure that you are not buying refined white sugar dyed brown.

Store sugar in an airtight glass container and keep it in a dry, cool part of the kitchen, away from steam.

Honey. There are many varieties of honey, including clover, orange and acacia, and the nutrients will vary according to the type you buy, and the soil conditions the plant grew in. Usually, though, honey contains vitamins B and C and minerals such as calcium, iron and silica. It is sold in liquid or solid form and even sometimes with its honeycomb, but this is expensive. If you use honey to sweeten cooked desserts, add it after cooking to prevent the nutrients being destroyed by the heat.

Honey will keep for a couple of months at room temperature but will crystallise if kept too long. Liquid honey will set if kept in the fridge.

Although these sugar alternatives contain more nutrients than pure white sugar, they do have the same calorific value and so are just as fattening as white sugar and should be used sparingly. Try to reduce your sugar consumption overall, by avoiding all commercially produced foods, including fizzy drinks and sweets. Do your own baking and eat a balanced wholefood diet as recommended in Chapter 9. In this way, all your energy needs are met by healthy carbohydrates and fats.

Alternative sweeteners. Avoid these at all costs. Most brands are made from synthetic substances such as coal-tar derivatives, and although we cannot be certain of the effect they have on our health, they are thought by some researchers to be harmful in the long term and linked with types of cancer. They also do nothing to educate the palate to prefer wholesome foods.

5

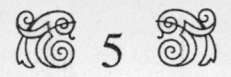

Fats

Fat provides a compact source of energy and we need it to maintain health and to give us healthy bones, teeth and skin. It comes, as we have already seen, from two sources: saturated fat from animals – butter, lard, dripping and suet; and polyunsaturated fats from vegetable and plant oils – sunflower oil, sesame seed oil, corn oil and olive oil, plus soft margarines made from these oils.

Most of us eat more fat than we need and nutritionists recommend that we reduce our daily intake to between 1 and 2 oz (25–50 g) a day, depending on our age and occupation. And most of that fat should be from polyunsaturated sources. If you are elderly, overweight or suffering from heart disease, then cut out all animal fat, including butter, and use cold-pressed vegetable oils and soft margarines instead. If, on the other hand, you are slim, healthy and have a balanced wholefood diet rich in fibre and wholegrains, then a little animal fat, like butter, does not present the same risk to health.

Butter
Butter is made from cream or the fatty droplets of milk and contains mostly saturated animal fat, fat-soluble vitamins A and D, and a tiny amount of milk sugar and milk protein.

There is a wide range of butter on sale in the shops, ranging in quality from pure dairy butter to blends of differing qualities, either salted or unsalted. The best choice would be a pure unsalted dairy butter, used sparingly on your bread or toast, just a scraping, rather than a thick layer.

If you are healthy and eat a wholefood diet, the choice between butter and margarine is reduced to a question of saturated fatty acids versus additives and personally I would choose butter every time because it is a more natural food and contains no additives.

Butter will keep indefinitely in the fridge or a cool dark place. When buying butter in bulk, freeze what you don't use.

Suet, lard and dripping
These are mainly unrefined saturated fatty acids and have little nutritional value. Use them sparingly or, if possible, cut them out of your diet altogether.

Margarines
Margarines are made from the fat of meat or fish or vegetables and are very often a blend of all three. They contain mainly unsaturated fatty acids with some saturated fatty acids. A culture of pasteurised milk is added, together with synthetic vitamins A and D, to give the equivalent vitamin value of butter. Other additives are then mixed with the fats to provide taste, colour and texture. Emulsifiers are also added to prevent the fat and liquid from separating.

Hard margarine has been hydrogenated to solidify the vegetable oils and this process changes the polyunsaturated fatty acids into saturated ones. However, since the discovery that polyunsaturated fatty acids from vegetable oils reduces cholesterol levels in the bloodstream, margarine manufacturers have found a way of making soft margarine entirely from vegetable oils without heating or hydrogenating the oil. In this way, the oil remains polyunsaturated. The most widely sold soft margarine in Britain is Flora, but healthfood shops stock other brands such as Lin-O-Saf made from safflower oil and Sun-O-Life made from sunflower oil.

Keep margarines in the fridge or a cool dark place and use them for cooking or spreading in place of butter.

Cooking fats
These are blends of oils and/or fats, which have been treated and texturised in the same way as hard margarines and so lack essential unsaturated fatty acids. They have no food value.

Vegetable oils
These are extracted from the seedgerm or fruit of various plants and are high in polyunsaturated fatty acids and contain vitamins A and D. The seedgerm oils also contain vitamin E, necessary to keep the reproductive system and heart functioning properly.

Sunflower, safflower and sesame seed oils are the best for cooking and, together with olive oil, are also valuable salad oils. Store the oils in a cool dark cupboard rather than in the fridge, where they may congeal. Never put used oil back into the bottle with unused oil. Strain used oil and keep it in a separate container. Cook food in oil on a very low heat to prevent the oil from turning into saturated fat.

Choose a cold-pressed unrefined vegetable oil for cooking. Oils extracted by a heat process have been changed into saturated fatty acids, so read the labels on the bottles carefully. Cold-pressed oils tend to be a little more expensive than refined oils extracted by heat, but from a nutritional point of view they are more healthy and worth the extra few pence.

Here is a brief guide on how to use fats in a healthy diet:

▷ Use a little butter, or soft margarine, or nut butter for spreading and baking.

▷ Use a cold-pressed vegetable oil for salad dressings, frying and baking. Check recipes for quantities.

▷ Fry food in a little cold-pressed oil and butter. The mixture of the two gives a good flavour and prevents the butter from burning.

Re-use the oil a few times, but do not overdo it, as it loses its nutritional value with constant use.

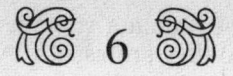

Vegetables and Fruit

Many fruits and vegetables contain protein, carbohydrate and fatty acids in very small quantities, but we use them principally as a source of fibre, vitamins and minerals. To ensure that we get all the minerals and vitamins that we need, nutritionists recommend that we eat a selection of fresh vegetables and fruit every day, in as near to their natural state as possible, that is, raw or lightly cooked, to take full advantage of the nutrients. In fact, it is recommended that one-third to one-half of our food be eaten raw. We can do this by having muesli, fruit and nuts for breakfast; a salad for lunch, and one, or two, lightly cooked vegetables with fruit at the evening meal.

Every day have a serving of a lightly cooked green vegetable, such as cabbage, broccoli, kale, watercress, Brussels sprouts or nettle tops, plus a serving of an orange or red vegetable such as carrots, tomatoes or red pepper. This provides a wide range of vital nutrients, including vitamins A and C, together with many minerals. The rest can be made up from other foods including fruit and a mixed salad.

Serve onions, leeks or garlic as often as possible to help prevent infections such as colds and coughs.

Try to have one of the citrus fruits – oranges, lemons and grapefruit – every day to provide you with vitamin C. Pure fruit juices sold in supermarkets are convenient and valuable, but squeeze your own fruit if you can, as it is fresher, or eat the whole fruit to get the fibre as well.

Apples and grapes contain vitamins A, B and C, plus many minerals, and they are usually available for most of the year. Try to have one of these fruits every day, and also make full use of the seasonal fruits.

The ways in which fruit and vegetables are selected, stored and cooked also affect the nutritional content and so all this must be done carefully.

If you can, grown your own vegetables and fruit, using organic methods rather than chemicals. Use compost, manure, or blood and bone as a fertiliser. Control pests by encouraging natural predators such as ladybirds and frogs, or by using natural pesticides, such as pyrethrum or tobacco juice. The latter is made by boiling 1 oz (25 g) tobacco dust in 2½ pints (1.4 litres) water for thirty minutes. Strain and bottle. Label clearly and keep out of the reach of children. Spray on these pesticides three clear weeks before you intend to harvest the plant. Your own produce may not be as large as the commercially grown varieties, but it will be cheaper, tastier and free from chemicals. If growing your own is not possible, find an organic market gardener or greengrocer in your area. If there is not one, buy your fruit and vegetables from a greengrocer rather than a supermarket. Food from a greengrocer's is normally fresher, less expensive, and unwashed, and so it will have retained more of its nutrients.

Make sure that the greengrocer has his shop in a side street or well back from the road, and buy produce from inside the shop rather than from outside displays, to avoid the inevitable coating of lead-bearing exhaust fumes from passing traffic.

Buy produce in season, when it is cheaper and fresher than tinned, dried or frozen fruit and vegetables. Any handling and preparation done before it reaches you means a loss of nutrients, even with frozen vegetables, which is the least damaging method of preserving food. As there is a steady loss of vitamin C, do not keep frozen vegetables in the freezer for too long.

Buy a variety of produce in small quantities, enough for say two to three days. This quick turnover will mean fresher food. And make sure it is fresh and not bruised or damaged in any way. Skins should be firm, not wrinkled, colours fresh, and green vegetables such as cabbage should have firm green leaves, not yellowing ones.

In the autumn there is the bonus of fruit from the hedgerows – blackberries, elderberries, rosehips and perhaps even damsons or apples from abandoned orchards. These are free and can be preserved to use during the winter in pies, tarts and drinks.

Store cucumbers, carrots, red and green peppers and other highly perishable vegetables in paper bags in the salad drawer of the fridge. Sprinkle lettuce with water and keep it in an open plastic bag in the fridge. Place watercress in a jug of cold water and store in the fridge. Use it before it turns yellow. Put green vegetables in a plastic bag in the fridge to prevent oxidation, which breaks down the nutrients. Root vegetables such as potatoes, swedes and parsnips are best stored in a cool, dark cupboard. Keep soft fruit like plums and grapes in a cool place and eat them within a few days. Citrus fruit and apples will keep longer.

Clean fruit and salad vegetables by rinsing them quickly in cold water. Shake them dry or wipe gently with a tea towel. Never leave them to soak or clean them in hot water, as this washes away much of their food value.

Scrub root vegetables such as carrots and potatoes and try, whenever possible, to retain their skins. This provides extra fibre and nutrients. Bake potatoes in their jackets. Add them to casseroles with their skins on. Do the same when frying potatoes. For mashed potato, boil them in their jackets and peel them afterwards. The skin will peel off quite easily, leaving the nutrients, which are just under the skin, intact.

Use the outer leaves of cabbage and lettuce whenever possible, as they contain more nutrients than the younger leaves. Most of the nutrients are retained if cooked vegetables are crisp yet tender; steaming in a pressure cooker or baking are the two best ways of achieving this. When boiling, plunge the vegetables into a little boiling water and cook with the lid firmly on for a few minutes. Turn the heat right down when the water has returned to the boil, and simmer. Then remove from the heat when the vegetable is slightly tender.

Save cooking water for soups, stocks and gravies so that none of the vegetables' nutrients are lost. Do not add salt to cooking water (it toughens some vegetables such as beans) and avoid bicarbonate of soda as it destroys vitamins B and C.

Cook fruit very briefly in a tiny amount of water. Try to serve cooked food immediately, to prevent further loss of nutrients.

Salads
Include a mixed salad in your daily menus to provide a range of nutrients. One useful guide is to have ingredients that represent the whole plant. For instance, carrots or beetroot represent the root; white cabbage, watercress or lettuce, the leaf; celery, the stalk; tomato, cucumber or green/red pepper, the fruit; broccoli or cauliflower, the flower; and perhaps add a sprinkling of nuts on special occasions to represent the seeds.

Freshly chopped or green-dried herbs, such as chives, parsley and basil (see Chapter 7) increase the flavour and value of the salad.

Prepare salads just before serving, if possible. If not, toss the salad vegetables (with the exception of the lettuce) in oil to seal in the nutrients, and place in the fridge. Add the lettuce and the rest of the dressing just before serving. The oil is also valuable in helping the body absorb the oil-soluble vitamins.

Although salad vegetables become scarcer and more expensive during the winter months, it is still possible to continue with a daily salad, using alternative vegetables such as cabbage, or hot-house lettuce, raw Brussels sprouts, peppers, sweet corn, apples and nuts. Beans and orange segments add a touch of colour to brighten up dull days, and you could even sprout your own beans, which are rich in vitamins, protein and minerals (see salad recipes).

7

Herbs

Many of the herbs that we now take for granted such as sage, rosemary and thyme, came originally from the dry, rocky areas of the Mediterranean. They were brought over to Britain by the Romans during their occupation from the first to the fourth centuries and were used to flavour their food and cure their ills.

Later, monks used them in their healing ministry, dispensing remedies made from herbs which they grew in intricate patterns based on the cross.

At about this time herbs also became a very important part of daily life in the manor houses and were used for everything from removing freckles to flavouring food. After the monasteries had been dissolved by Henry VIII in the 1530s, the lady of the manor also took over the role of healing the sick.

Among the keys attached to her belt, every chatelaine had a key to the distilling room where she distilled her own essences from the herbs which she grew in her elaborate garden. There gardens were planted with the old-fashioned flowers and herbs, carnations, foxgloves, roses, hyssop, peonies and thyme, which were arranged to attract the bees. The gardens were a focal point of the daily constitutional of members of the household, a quiet place where people could be soothed by the beauty and fragrance of the flowers.

The scene gradually changed in the eighteenth and nineteenth centuries, once the Industrial Revolution got under way. The use of fresh rather than preserved meat, as a result of refrigeration, reduced the need for herbs, as did the introduction of alternative disinfectants, cleansers and synthetic medicines based on coal derivatives. So herbs receded into the background, relegated to culinary garnishes like stuffings and flavourings for sauces.

In recent years, I am glad to say, herbs seem to be making a comeback on all fronts, including food, and there are many varieties available, fresh or dried, with plenty of advice on how to use them.

Herbs are best used fresh and so if you have the space, and inclination, try cultivating your own. Grow them in a little patch near the back door, so that you don't have far to go for a sprig of this or that. Most are easy to grow and need little attention, just a sunny, well-drained position and regular watering for most, and partial shade and moist conditions for parsley, chervil and chives. If you have no garden, they will grow equally well in window boxes or pots.

Thyme, parsley and other perennials can be used all the year round, but others, like basil, are annuals and so to use them during the winter, the leaves will have to be frozen, or dried by hanging the stems in loose bunches upside down in a dark, warm dry place such as the airing cupboard. They should then be crumbled and stored in glass jars in a cool, dark spot in the kitchen.

Most herbs freeze extremely well and can be kept in the freezer for up to one year. When freezing, remove the leaves from the stem, leave the leaves whole, and place in small quantities, a few leaves at a time, sufficient for one meal, in small plastic bags, or pieces of plastic film. They will not look as attractive as the fresh herb, but they will be just as aromatic and nutritious.

If it is impossible to grow your own herbs, then buy them dried from healthfood shops, which usually stock a wide range. When choosing your herbs, avoid those that look straw-coloured. Herbs should be green when dried and should look as near as possible to their original colour. If they do not, then they have been badly dried or have been kept too long, and either way will have lost their potency and should not be bought. Buy them an ounce at a time, unless you intend to use large quantities, and store the herbs in glass jars in a cool, dark place. Replace the herbs after a year as all the taste and goodness will have been lost and they will taste and smell like stale tobacco.

Herbs add more than a special flavour to food: they contain vitamins and minerals, which makes them a valuable dietary supplement. Here are a few herbs that you can experiment with.

Basil
This is the king of herbs for me. It has a wonderful flavour and Italians use it liberally in many of their dishes to give them that distinctive flavour. It goes exceptionally well with tomatoes and a simple salad of sliced tomatoes sprinkled with freshly chopped basil is delectable. It also goes well with egg and cheese dishes, can be added to French dressing and used with poultry and fish such as mackerel and sole. This herb is best used fresh or frozen. Use it sparingly to begin with until you are familiar with its flavour.

Bay leaves
These are a necessary ingredient in bouquets garnis, used in France to flavour stocks, stews and casseroles. They go well with most meats, poultry and fish and can be added to cooking vegetables to add a subtle flavour. This herb is generally used dried and should be used cautiously to begin with until you are used to its strength.

Celery leaves
These have a subtle flavour and can be used lavishly, dried or fresh. They go well with most soups, sauces and stews and impart a special flavour to salads, cheese and egg dishes.

Chives
Chives can be used dried, but are best fresh. They have a

mild onion flavour and can be used generously in most dishes, for example, in salads, vegetables, cheese, omelettes, soups, potatoes, sauces, savoury pancakes. They go particularly well with cottage cheese and cream cheese.

Fennel
This is a frondy herb with a slightly aniseed flavour. The parts used are the leaves and seeds. It is best used fresh, but can be dried. Use it sparingly to begin with. It especially suits oily fish, such as mackerel, and goes well with salads, soups and stews. It also adds a special flavour to egg dishes.

Lemon Balm
As its name suggests, this herb has a lemony flavour and is best used fresh. It can be used to flavour almost any dish.

Marjoram (sweet)
This is another herb much used in Italian dishes. It has a strong aromatic flavour and should be used sparingly, either dried or fresh. It suits strongly flavoured meats such as beef, rabbit or pork.

The Mints
There are a number in this family, including spearmint, peppermint and bowles. The one commonly used in cooking is the spearmint. It suits fatty meats such as lamb and roast beef and can enhance the flavour of vegetables, particularly peas and potatoes. Use this herb sparingly, fresh or dried.

Parsley
This delicately flavoured herb is rich in vitamin C and calcium and can be used lavishly, fresh or dried. It goes well with most savoury dishes.

Rosemary
Rosemary is a strong aromatic herb and should be used sparingly, dried or fresh. It enhances the flavour of meat

dishes, in particular soups, stews and casseroles and will also add extra flavour to beans, peas and baked potatoes.

Sage
This makes an ideal poultry stuffing and goes well with egg and cheese dishes, especially omelettes and scrambled eggs. It will enhance the flavour of most meat dishes and of some vegetables, such as beans, spinach, aubergines and pulses. Use it sparingly, dried or fresh.

Summer Savory
Summer savory has a strong flavour and should be used carefully to begin with. Used dried or fresh, it can be added to all roast meat dishes, in chicken stuffings or rabbit stews. Add it to the cooking water of broad beans, French and runner beans, cabbage, peas and haricot beans, to give them a special flavour.

Tarragon
This is an important ingredient in 'fines herbes' and is used to flavour omelettes, stuffings and marinades. Add it to French dressings and sprinkle on green salads. It goes well with poultry and fish and is excellent with steaks and grilled fish. Use it sparingly, fresh or dried.

Thyme
Thyme is a strong aromatic herb and another essential ingredient in bouquets garnis. Use it carefully, dried or fresh. It goes well with meat such as mutton or pork, and can be used in thick soups and stews. It also goes well with some oily fish like mackerel, eels and all shellfish.

Bouquet garni
This can be made easily, either by tying together a sprig of fresh thyme, parsley and bay leaf, or by putting a flat teaspoon of each dried crumbled herb into a small square of muslin. Tie with a piece of cotton and add to the pot.

Remove just before serving.

Fines herbes
This is a French culinary term for an equal mixture of chives, parsley, chervil and tarragon which is used to flavour grilled meat, omelettes, soups and sauces. The herbs can be used dried, but are better when fresh or frozen.

Then there are the wild herbs. They do not have the strong aromatic flavour of their cultivated cousins, but they do have fine food value and are a good source of vitamins and minerals.

Nettle
The young tops can be picked before flowering (wear gloves!) and used as a substitute for spinach. Cook them in exactly the same way. Alternatively, dry them and spinkle over most dishes. Nettle has a very mild flavour, but is rich in iron and silicic acid.

Dandelion leaves
The young leaves can be used raw in salads and are high in vitamins A, B, C and D and some minerals such as potassium.

Milfoil (Yarrow)
This frondy herb can be used in exactly the same way as nettle and dandelion leaves, sprinkled over foods and added to salads.

Elderflowers
During the late spring use these to flavour drinks, cakes and puddings such as pancakes.

Further Reading

Grieve, M., *A Modern Herbal*. Penguin 1980.
Hall, Dorothy, *The Book of Herbs*. Pan 1972.

Loewenfeld, Claire and Back, Philippa, *Herbs for Health and Cookery*. Pan 1965.

8

Drinks

Our bodies are two-thirds water and need regular supplies of fluid to work efficiently. So although we can live several weeks without food, we would die of thirst within a few days without water.

In the Bible, fasting usually refers to going without food. Absolute fasts (that is, going without food *and* drink) were rare, and even then, usually lasted for three days at the most (Esther 4.16 and Acts 9.9). Absolute fasts for longer periods than that, such as Moses' fast of forty days (Exodus 34.28) were very rare and were only carried out under God's specific guidance.

Not only is water important to us, but what we add to it is also important, because these additives can feed or harm the body, depending upon what they are. If we intend to eat properly, it is necessary to examine our drinking habits to make sure that they are not undermining our healthy eating plan.

To help you in this, here is a brief survey of the usual drinks found in most homes together with some suggested alternatives.

Coffee and tea

These are relative newcomers to the refreshment scene, first being introduced to Europe in the seventeenth century by the merchant traders. For a couple of centuries they remained a luxury for the rich, but have since percolated down to within the reach of the rest of us and have become closely woven into the social fabric of our society. Tea and coffee breaks wouldn't be the same without them, nor would church socials and coffee mornings!

Although these drinks are quick and easy to prepare, and help to feed relationships, they do nothing to feed our bodies. In fact, the presence of tannin and caffeine in both drinks can be harmful. Tannin gives the drink its strength and body, but can cause heartburn and indigestion by increasing the concentration of hydrochloric acid in the stomach. Caffeine gives us the 'lift' we need, but if taken regularly in large quantities it can produce worrying side effects that include irritability, anxiety, nervousness, dizzy spells, irregular heartbeat, increased blood pressure and pulse rate and hand tremors. As if that is not enough, caffeine is also a diuretic – it causes an excessive loss of fluid from the body, and hence a loss of valuable supplies of B vitamins, which can lead to premature baldness and greying of hair in some people.

It is difficult to say how much is too much; this depends largely on our metabolism and the strength and size of the cup of coffee or tea. But a rough guide would be one to two cups a day; anything over that could be harmful.

Do not give these drinks to children, and try to reduce your own consumption by gradually changing over to nutritious substitutes, such as dandelion coffee and herbal teas, which are discussed at the end of the chapter.

Decaffeinated coffee is merely coffee without the caffeine. It has no nutritional value.

Cocoa and malted bedtime drinks
These contain large amounts of carbohydrate and fat and so tend to be very fattening. Most preparations also contain additives and sugar which only make a fattening situation worse. You would be far better off with a cup of hot milk, or a soothing herbal tea, such as chamomile or elderflower.

Water and mineral waters
Tap water can be hard or soft, depending on the area you

live in, and whilst both have benefits, from a health point of view, hard water is the more beneficial (even if it does fur up the kettle!) because it contains minerals which soft water does not. As well as its natural qualities, tap water also contains chemicals such as chlorine and fluorine, added by the water boards to purify the water and prevent tooth decay. These are considered to be pollutants by some.

Streams and wells are often affected by chemical run-offs from agricultural land or industrial waste and even by exhaust fumes from traffic.

About the only untainted water source is mineral water from deep underground springs, which contains a host of minerals, most of which are beneficial to health. 'Taking the water' at spa towns like Bath or Tunbridge Wells was a favourite pastime of the eighteenth century rich, who used them as we use health farms today to repair some of the damage done during the year by excessive eating and drinking. They fell out of fashion during the nineteenth century in favour of seaside resorts like Brighton, but fortunately there is now a growing revival of interest in mineral water, and genuine mineral waters from England and the Continent are becoming increasingly available at reasonable prices. They can be bought at most off-licences and supermarkets.

Alcohol

Hard spirits, such as gin and whisky, have the same stimulating and diuretic qualities as coffee and tea and they irritate the digestive tract, too. They are rich in empty calories and so are fattening, whilst reducing the appetite for nutritious food at the same time. An excess of alcohol taken over a period of time causes more than hangovers – it can do serious damage to the liver.

If you drink alcohol, avoid hard spirits and stick to moderate amounts of wine (especially dry white wine which is non-fattening), cider and beer (although beer is very fattening, containing 220 calories per pint), all of which contain vitamins and minerals that will help to feed the body.

Soft drinks
Colas and squashes and other synthetic soft drinks are chemical brews of colour additives, sweeteners, flavourings, fizz and preservatives. They have no nutrients and sometimes have been nowhere near the fruit they represent. The high sugar content makes them fattening and harmful to the teeth and if given to children will also encourage a taste for sweet things that can last for life.

Instead, squeeze your own fruits, or make some homemade drinks from the recipe section of this book. If that is not possible, make more use of pure fruit and vegetable juices which are additive free, and available in most supermarkets and healthfood shops. These are a valuable food source and help to cleanse the body, build up new cells and maintain health.

SUGGESTED ALTERNATIVES

Coffee substitutes
▷ Dandelion coffee made from the roasted roots of the dandelion plant. It contains vitamins A and C and a variety of minerals including, calcium, magnesium and silicon.

▷ Barley Cup, made from wholegrain barley.

▷ Cider vinegar and honey. This is full of minerals such as magnesium, sulphur and iron. Make it by adding one dessertspoon of cider vinegar to a glass of hot water and sweeten with honey as desired.

Herbal teas
These are refreshing and contain volatile oils, minerals and vitamins that help the body to function properly. An increasing range of dried herbs is available in healthfood

shops and these can be used as teas, or for many other reasons, such as the treatment of minor ailments like coughs and colds and as cosmetics.

If taken regularly, and depending on the herb you use, you will usually notice beneficial side effects such as calmer nerves, clearer skins or glossier hair. Here are just a few suggested herbal teas:

▷ Rosehip, hibiscus flowers, lemon balm, raspberry leaves, blackberry leaves, lime flowers. All have a refreshing and sometimes tart flavour and can be taken at any time.

▷ Nettle, sage, rosemary. These are tonics and are best taken during the day, preferably in the morning.

▷ Peppermint, chamomile, fennel seed and dill seed. These are fine after-dinner digestives.

▷ Elderflower, chamomile, fennel and dill seeds. These make soothing bedtime drinks.

▷ Yarrow and chamomile are useful teas for convalescents, as they speed up the recovery process.

Make the tea by allowing one teaspoon dried (1 tablespoon fresh) herb per person and one for the pot. Infuse for five to eight minutes and strain. Sweeten with honey or sweet cicely, if desired. See Chapter 7 for hints on buying herbs.

Fruit and vegetable juices
Fruit juices can be bought easily in most shops, but vegetable juices are scarcer and may have to be made at home. This is done quite easily if you have an electric liquidiser.

Suitable vegetables are: most leaf, root and tuberous vegetables. The most nutritious and flavourful are: carrots, tomatoes, beetroots, white radishes, cabbage, celery, spinach and cucumber. They can be blended to suit individual tastes and to give a fuller range of nutrients.

Preparation. Wash or scrub the vegetables. Chop them into small pieces and liquidise with a little water. Add herbs to flavour and soften the taste of tart vegetables, or use the top of the milk or cereal cream.

Useful herbs to flavour juices. Celery leaves, chives, parsley, basil, lovage, chervil and tarragon.

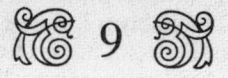

Changing to a Wholefood Diet

It is quite easy for single people to change their diet to wholefoods. All they need is some basic knowledge of food values and the motivation to eat properly, and they are on their way to better health. But when there are other people to consider, it may not be quite so simple. Husbands and children brought up on one type of food may be resistant, at first, to the idea that wholefoods are a change for the better. They will probably have preconceived notions about health food, that it is 'rabbit's food' or 'tastes like sawdust'. They may even point to Great Aunt Agatha who lived an active life until she was a hundred and three on white bread, fried foods and coffee, and argue that what is good enough for her is fine for them.

Children, especially, tend to have very conservative eating habits and if they have been used to fish fingers, white bread, crisps and fizzy drinks for most of their lives, they might need some persuasion to change to wholefoods.

For these reasons it is necessary to have clear reasons for changing your diet so that when opposition comes (or *if* it comes, because there is always the delightful possibility that there will not be any) your commitment and motivation will be strong enough to persuade your family of the error of their thinking.

Study the Bible and learn for yourself what it says about stewardship of the earth, our bodies and the needy. Then, in the light of what you read, prayerfully examine your own life, diet and lifestyle. Ask yourself some searching questions. Am I being a responsible steward of the land, my body and my neighbour? Am I feeding my family properly? What are the weak areas in our diet and how can they be improved? Am I spending my housekeeping money wisely? Is there any unnecessary waste? Find out more about present land use and Third World issues. Discover the needs of people in the Third World, how they are being met and by whom.

If your children are old enough to understand, explain your reasons for changing your diet and get their co-operation. I often think that we underestimate a child's ability to understand important issues, and very often they are much more co-operative if they can see the reason for something. It could be a great adventure for them. They could be involved in planning the menu, or the shopping, even the cooking. In this way you can teach them the rudiments of cookery, the basics of healthy eating and the principles of housekeeping, all of which will be useful when they leave home. On rainy days and flat moments, one friend cooks for the freezer with her two-year-old son. He enjoys this immensely and takes much more interest in his food when he has helped to prepare it himself.

If you do have a family, do not change your diet overnight. Expect eating habits to change slowly. This gives you time to build up knowledge and expertise, and your family time to digest a new idea and get used to it. Sudden drastic changes in diet could overwhelm them and put them off wholefoods for life.

Do not worry if some new dishes are rejected the first or second time they are introduced. Try them again later. It is more than likely that the family will soon learn to enjoy them. There are not that many dishes which children reject once they are familiar with them, especially if they are attractively presented.

Good presentation is a necessary part of any meal. It stimulates the appetite and digestive juices, as well as adding to the enjoyment of a meal. And it is an important way to counter the image of wholefoods as dull and tasteless.

Wholefoods are appetising and satisfying and should reflect this in their appearance.

If we have always eaten what we fancy, the palate will have become dulled and will need more and more exotic dishes to stimulate the taste buds. But if we simplify our diet, and make it more wholesome, eating according to need rather than greed, all that will vanish. Jaded palates are revitalised and we can appreciate celebratory meals to the full. Birthdays, wedding anniversaries and visits from relatives or friends are all opportunities to celebrate with a special meal. We need not feel guilty about this: Jesus enjoyed special meals with friends (Luke 10.38–42) and even the poorest communities have regular feasts and festivals. But space them out so that they are used to mark special events and remain 'occasions'.

Once you have gained your family's co-operation and enthusiasm, commit your new diet and housekeeping plans to God, ask his blessing and guidance and then gradually reform your diet. Here are some ways of doing it.

Reducing salt

▷ You can eliminate a large quantity of salt in your diet if you stop eating convenience foods; for example, tinned foods such as spaghetti, beans and vegetables, pies and frozen meals. Do this gradually.

▷ Replace stock cubes, tinned or packeted soups and savoury drinks, with homemade equivalents, using little or no salt. They will usually freeze well and have more flavour.

▷ Do your own baking and reduce, or leave out, the salt.

▷ Do not add salt to your cooking water, and when the food is on the table taste it first to see if extra salt is needed. Even then use the salt shaker sparingly. Cut out salt altogether if you can, and make more use of herbal seasoning (see Chapter 7).

▷ Avoid salted meats like bacon.

▷ Replace crisps and other salted savoury snacks with nuts and raisins or fruit and raw vegetables.

▷ Make sure that the salt you do use is sea salt. It is purer than rock salt and, like seafood, contains iodine which is necessary to keep the thyroid gland functioning properly.

Reducing sugar

▷ Phase out tinned foods, such as fruit and vegetables, most of which, together with convenience foods such as pies and pastries, have hidden sugar. Use fresh foods instead.

▷ Make your own cakes and puddings, and reduce the amount of sugar suggested in the recipes to a level that your family finds acceptable.

▷ Ban refined white sugar, except when there is no suitable alternative, and sweeten with honey, malt extract or other unrefined sweeteners. But use the sweetener sparingly, for it has the same calorific value as refined sugar.

▷ Use fresh fruit juices in place of manufactured soft drinks. Add sparkling mineral water if children like their drinks fizzy.

▷ Make milkshakes from fresh milk. Add fresh fruit purées, or carob powder (instead of chocolate) for flavour.

▷ Phase out sweets and replace them with fruit and nuts, sunflower seeds and sticks of raw vegetables.

▷ Avoid all cake mixes and packeted desserts and eat more fruit salads, yoghurt and milk puddings instead.

▷ Phase out sugar in hot drinks.

▷ During the summer, make your own ice cream and serve fresh fruit drinks from freshly squeezed or puréed fruit.

▷ Make your own ice lollies, too, by freezing fruit juice in ice cube moulds. Add yoghurt to increase nutrition and variety, and insert toothpicks when the ice has almost set. These ice lollies are much cheaper and tastier than the shop-bought ones.

Reducing fat
Bearing in mind that we do need a small amount of fat each day, here are some ways of reducing fat intake if it is too high.

▷ Avoid processed and manufactured foods, including sausages, pork pies and other similar foods.

▷ Reduce fried meals to one to three times a week and regularly replace chips with a baked potato.

▷ Eat less meat, trim off the excess fat and make more use of fish and pulses.

▷ Cook with vegetable oils rather than animal fat.

▷ Use yoghurt instead of cream, and cottage cheese in place of cream cheese (although do not cut them out altogether – treat yourself sometimes).

▷ Cut out all fried savoury snacks, like crisps. On the days when you do not have fried foods, get your daily fat from butter or soft margarine, cheese and salad dressings.

Increase your fibre
▷ Change to wholemeal bread, and bake your own. As wholemeal bread can be heavier than the white fluff we normally eat, break in the family's digestive system gently by baking with 50 per cent white flour and 50 per cent wholemeal and gradually increase the wholemeal over a period of time.

- ▷ Eat homemade muesli (see recipe, p. 137) in place of packeted cereals.
- ▷ Add extra bran and wheatgerm to crumbles and pastries.
- ▷ Make your own breadcrumbs, using wholemeal bread.
- ▷ Eat plenty of fresh fruit and vegetables, leaving the skins on wherever practicable, and eat a daily salad of raw vegetables. Cook vegetables briefly in a little water until they are tender, but crisp.
- ▷ Use wholemeal pasta and noodles, and make more use of pulses, unpolished rice and potatoes baked in their jackets.

Avoid additives

- ▷ This is easily done if you cut out all processed and packeted foods, including commercially made pâtés, sausages, yoghurts, drinks, etc.
- ▷ Make your own sauces and salad dressings.
- ▷ Make your own crumbles, custards and stuffings, as well as your own cakes, pastries and desserts. Many of these can be made in bulk and frozen to save time and effort later on.

If ever you feel your resolve flagging and you are tempted to go back to your old eating pattern, encourage yourself by knowing that you are feeding your family a healthy diet, and are using God's resources wisely, too. Added encouragement will come as you notice a correction in your weight and an improvement in your health and the health of your family. Those persistent colds and coughs should become scarcer. You will also feel more alert and energetic, and this will enhance your spiritual life.

I found that cooking for a wholefood diet became a creative challenge rather than a chore. It was fun, and still is, trying out new recipes. There were failures which became huge successes after a little practice, whilst others were never tried again.

You will also be heartened by the financial savings because, contrary to belief, a wholefood diet is less expensive than a refined diet. Once you have adjusted to the new way of eating, you will consume less because the body will be getting more of the nutrients that it needs. There are long term benefits too – as your health increases, there will be fewer doctor's and dentist's bills.

10

Planning and Budgeting a Menu

One helpful way of ensuring a smooth transition from refined foods to wholefoods is to sit down and prepare your menus in advance, either for the week or, preferably, for the coming month.

Write them out on a piece of paper, putting down what you will have for breakfast, lunch and the evening meal. Juggle the dishes to get the full range of nutrients at each meal to keep you vital and satisfied during the day, and plan for variety too. This will be necessary if you wish to convert the family successfully to wholefoods. Have meat for the main meal one day, a rice dish the next and fish the day after. In this way you are making full use of the protein sources whilst reducing your meat consumption.

Serve the foods in the correct quantities for the age and occupation of the members in your family. This will, in the long run, save money and prevent waste – an important consideration at a time when the hunger gap between the North and South is widening. It is not enough to fast occasionally and give away the cost of the meal. We need to make these fundamental changes in our diet to take the strain of overproduction off the land and make more money available to the needy to finance local agricultural schemes so that they can have a greater share in the earth's abundance.

To help you plan your menus effectively, here is a summary of the basic nutrients that the body needs each day.

Protein from meat, fish, poultry, eggs, milk, cheese and pulses.

Carbohydrates from wholewheat bread, wholegrain cereals, potatoes, pasta, unpolished rice, honey, molasses etc.

Fats from butter, meat, soft margarine, vegetable oils.

Fibre from wholegrain breads, cereals, fruit and vegetables.

Vitamins: A from fish liver oil, green and yellow fruit and vegetables. B from wholegrain bread and cereals, wheatgerm, brewer's yeast and blackstrap molasses. Riboflavin from dairy produce and yeast extracts. Pyridoxine from liver, bran, vegetables and blackstrap molasses. Niacin from meat, bran, legumes, wholegrain cereals. C from green leafy vegetables, citrus fruit and parsley. D from fish and fish liver oil. E from wheatgerm, green leafy vegetables and plant oils. K from blackstrap molasses and green leafy vegetables.

Minerals: Calcium from milk, cheese, pulses, nuts and green leafy vegetables. Phosphorus from meat, milk, cheese, fish, eggs, wholewheat cereals, pulses. Iron from egg yolk, red meats, wheatgerm, green vegetables, wholegrain cereals. Copper from liver, egg yolk, nuts, bran, blackstrap molasses.

Trace elements mostly found in vegetables, blackstrap molasses and sea foods, i.e., fish, shell fish and seaweed.

If you have a little food from each of the four main food groups with each meal, i.e., protein, carbohydrate, fat, vitamins and minerals, your body will be getting all the nutrients that it needs to stay healthy.

Another effective use of food is to arrange the meals so that you have the bulk of your food when you are most active. For instance if you have a nine to five office job, eat a large breakfast, a medium-sized lunch and a small evening meal. In this way the body gets the nutrients it needs when it needs them. This keeps blood sugar levels constant and prevents mid-morning tiredness. If you have had a large meal late the night before, eat a small breakfast, as it is unlikely that you will be hungry. This will also help you to stay slim because the body will be using all the food it gets and there will be little or no excess to store as fat.

Eat plenty of fresh fruit and vegetables and try to eat between one third and half your food raw. This provides extra fibre and nutrients. If you intend to reduce your meat consumption, plan a substitute that has the equivalent amount of protein as a serving of meat.

Menu Outline

Here is a menu outline that will provide all the necessary nutrients needed each day. Choose one food from each section:

Breakfast
Fruit juice, fresh fruit, reconstituted fruit
Shredded wheat, muesli, porridge with milk, wholewheat pancakes with yoghurt
Eggs, fish, cheese, meat, yoghurt
Wholewheat bread or toast, buttered
Coffee substitute, herbal tea, milk for children

Lunch
Eggs (if none for breakfast) cheese, meat, fish, pulses
Wholewheat bread, roll, pastry
Mixed salad with dressing, watercress, celery, tomato, carrot
Fruit
Fruit and nuts, cake (optional extra)

Tea
A piece of fruit and herbal tea
For ravenous children home from school, savoury scones, wholemeal bread and a spread, fruit cake, flapjacks

Evening meal
Soup, salad, fruit juice
Fish, meat, pulses, cheese, eggs, rice
Green and yellow vegetables
Fruit or light dessert

This is just an outline and will have to be adjusted to suit particular needs. Children, for instance, will need more milk and energy-producing foods such as bread, cakes, etc., and if you are slimming or elderly, you may wish to cut out the desserts, except for special occasions.

The following sample menus for a week should help to get you started. They are based on recipes at the end of the book; I am assuming that the midday meal will be a packed lunch on most days.

▷ *Day 1*
 Breakfast   Fresh fruit juice
         Muesli with milk and half a sliced banana
         Scrambled egg with a pinch of sage and parsley
         A slice of wholewheat toast
         Herbal tea or coffee substitute, and milk for children.
 Lunch   A slice of Quiche Lorraine
         Wild herb salad with oil-based dressing
         Yoghurt
         An apple and an orange
 Evening meal Pistou soup
         Liver casserole, baked potato, buttered nettletops or spinach
         Baked banana

▷ *Day 2*
 Breakfast   Pancakes with yoghurt, fruit and nuts
         Herbal tea or coffee substitute, and milk for children
 Lunch   Scotch egg
         Slice wholemeal bread, buttered
         Bean sprout, mushroom and celery salad
         An apple and some grapes

Evening meal	Vegetarian roast, tomato sauce, steamed broccoli and glazed carrots, chive potato cakes Chocolate pudding

▷ **Day 3**

Breakfast	Fruit juice Muesli and milk, chopped apple Poached egg on wholewheat toast Herbal tea, coffee substitute, and milk for children
Lunch	Wholemeal sandwiches with cottage cheese filling, mixed with chives, parsley, red and green pepper, watercress A carrot and a stick of celery An apple and an orange
Evening meal	Avocado appetiser Fish flan with ratatouille Fresh fruit salad

▷ **Day 4**

Breakfast	Reconstituted dried fruit Muesli and milk, plus half a chopped apple Cheese and tomato on toast Herbal tea, coffee substitute, and milk for children
Lunch	Pasty Tomato, stick of celery and watercress An apple and grapes
Evening meal	Green salad Peanut paella, courgettes and glazed carrots Yoghurt

▷ Day 5
Breakfast	Muesli with fruit juice and chopped fruit glass of fortified milk (see recipe for liquid breakfast)
	A slice of wholemeal toast (optional)
Lunch	Potato and cheese turnover
	A slice of wholemeal bread, buttered
	Stick of celery and carrot and watercress
	An apple and some grapes
Evening meal	Apple, walnut and celery salad with dressing
	Rabbit casserole, glazed carrots and peas
	Baked banana and yoghurt

▷ Day 6
Breakfast	Half a grapefruit
	Banana ambrosia
	A slice of wholemeal toast, buttered
	Herbal tea, coffee substitute and milk for children.
Lunch	Country harvest soup
	Herb scones
	Wild herb salad
	An apple
Evening meal	Basil stuffed tomatoes
	Lasagne al forno, baked potato, green salad
	Crème caramel

▷ Day 7
Breakfast	Fruit juice
	Muesli, milk and sliced banana
	Fried egg and tomato with fried wholemeal bread
	Herbal tea, coffee substitute, and milk for children.

Lunch	Half a grapefruit
	Tarragon chicken, roast potatoes, roast parsnip, peas and carrots
	Rice pudding
Tea	Tuna fish salad
	Vanilla cheesecake

Budgeting a menu
Apart from the nutritional and financial benefits of planning meals, there are others too. For instance, you are freed from the daily chore of deciding what to eat. If you have written out your menus for the week or month and have it pinned up on the wall in the kitchen, all you need to do is to glance at the day's menu in the morning and get the meat, fish or (if you have done some bulk cooking) ready-prepared dish out of the freezer to defrost in the fridge. I find this very liberating. Obviously the system has its limitations, especially if friends drop in for a meal unexpectedly. This may upset the meal plan for the day, but it does not matter. Overall, planning menus relieves stress and saves a lot of time.

It makes shopping easier and more efficient, too. Once you know what you are going to eat you can draw up your shopping list from the menus. This helps to cut out that expensive last minute panic buying as you nip down to the corner shop at the end of the day to buy something quick, easy and expensive. If it is all there in the freezer or the cupboard, you are unlikely to run out of food at inconvenient moments.

Once I started advance planning in this way, after years of wasteful shopping, I was able to cut my food bills by a third and yet eat a more varied and nutritious diet than I had eaten previously, without stinting or denying myself in any way.

The weekly shopping basket will be lighter because you will have already bought the heavy goods, and you will spend less time shopping. Instead of trailing round the supermarket aisles looking for inspiration and being tempted by expensive foods that you do not really need, you can go straight to the relevant food counter and be out of the shop again before temptation gets its grip.

When making out my lists I have found that it helps to have a realistic budget (allowing extra for entertaining) and to keep a record of what I spend that money on. At the end of one month I plan the menus for the next and then make out five shopping lists. For the first list I scan the menus and make a list of all the dried goods I will need for one month – flour, rice, pasta, cereals, wheatgerm, bran, oats, dried fruit, nuts, skimmed milk powder, soya flour, shredded wheat, any tinned foods, herbs, margarine, oil, vinegar, sugar, honey, meat and fish (for the freezer). Plus other household items such as toilet paper and washing up liquid. I note the quantities I will need and then have a monthly bulk buying spree.

The other four weekly lists are made up from the menus and consist of the perishable foods I will need, such as bread (if it is bought), juice, fruit and vegetables.

This new habit will take a little time to acquire, and planning menus and budgets will be slow and experimental at first. But it will soon become easier as dishes and ingredients are repeated and so become standard. You will be delighted with the quick turnover of food and the reduction of waste.

Do not be too legalistic about your budgeting, though. There will be times when you have to overspend your budget or want to treat yourself and the family to a luxury. Do so and enjoy it: God wants us to enjoy the good things in his world, as long as we are looking after the needy too.

Further ways of cutting the cost and saving time and money

▷ *Shopping*

Compare the food prices in shops in your areas, if you don't already do so, and buy the most reasonably priced foods. 'Own brands' are usually cheaper than named brands, but are of the same quality.

Shop on a Thursday if possible. Food prices are often higher in some areas on a Friday or Saturday. This leaves your weekend free, too.

Buy dry goods such as flour, beans, oats etc., loose to avoid wasteful packaging.

Buy washing powders and other household items in economy sizes. They are usually cheaper and there is less wasteful packaging.

Whenever possible buy direct from a miller, farmer or organic gardener. The produce will be fresher and often cheaper than shopping through a retailer.

▷ *Fruit and vegetables*
Use seasonal fruits and vegetables rather than expensive frozen or tinned varieties. Make use of wild fruits and preserve them.

▷ *Meats*
Save expensive roasts and chops for special occasions and make more use of the cheaper meats such as liver, kidney, heart, oxtail, stewing steak, neck of lamb etc.

Combine small amounts of meat with rice (chicken paella), pasta (spaghetti bolognese) and beans (chilli con carne) to make it go further.

Make your own stock from meat bones (often given away free by butchers) and vegetable peelings.

▷ *Save time and money*
Make your own yoghurt, using a starter from a healthfood shop. Make your own dressings, mayonnaise, etc.
Make up a month's supply of pastry, dough, breadcrumbs, crumble, etc. and keep it in the freezer.

Make up a month's supply of muesli and store it in a jar in the food cupboard.

Have a bulk baking session once a month, cook pies, casseroles, beans, cakes, bread etc. and freeze them. When using the oven, make sure that it is full.

▷ *Gardening*
If you have the space, why not produce your own organically grown fruit and vegetables? Dig up a bit of your lawn and some of the flowerbeds at the bottom of the garden and grow some fruit and vegetables instead. There is little more satisfying than eating the fruits of your labours.

See p. 52 for some ideas about growing herbs. You could also try growing vegetables in pots, window boxes or growbags.

11

Nutrition for Special Situations

Most people can be greatly helped to better health by eating a wholefood diet as suggested in Chapters 9 and 10. If you have a specific problem, such as diabetes, heart disease or arthritis, you can also find relief through a wholefood diet, but you should consult a registered nutritionist who can plan a diet specifically to meet your needs.

There is another category of person though, who is not sick, but needs to adapt a wholefood diet to suit their particular circumstances and this is what we shall be looking at here.

Cooking in a Bedsitter
If you live in a bedsitter there is a great temptation to eat convenience foods. Restricted space, limited cooking facilities and the thought of sleeping with your cooking smells, all make it far easier to bring back a pie from the corner shop on the way home from work.

This is understandable, and it does make life a little easier in some ways. But it is an expensive way to eat and it doesn't provide all the nutrients that are needed to stay healthy. On the other hand, a little organisation and a working knowledge of food values will make it possible to eat extremely well and healthily, regardless of the size of the room and the facilities.

The key is to plan your meals on a weekly basis, taking into account nutrients, variety and your limited facilities. If these are very restricted and you have only a tiny working top and storage space, with a gas ring or two, plan simple but nourishing meals that need little or no cooking, or that can be cooked in one pan.

Drink pure fruit and vegetable juices, and eat lots of fresh fruit and salad vegetables, plus reconstituted dried fruit. This will supply your vitamin and mineral needs. You can sprout your own beans on the window sill (see p. 109), and keep potted plants of parsley and chives for extra flavour and minerals.

Make greater use of dairy products such as eggs, cheese and yoghurt for protein, and grill or fry fish, liver, kidney and lean minced meat; they are inexpensive and nourishing, but can be easily cooked without an oven. Treat yourself regularly to a rice or pasta dish with meat or vegetable sauces. You can make these easily in a couple of saucepans. Eat it with a green or mixed salad, or a steamed green vegetable.

Buy a ready made muesli without sugar from a healthfood shop, or make your own (see p. 137), and eat plenty of wholemeal bread, wholemeal pastas and unpolished rice, for carbohydrate and fibre. Get your extra fat from butter, soft margarine, vegetable cooking oil and salad dressings.

You could organise your menus something like this, choosing one from each section:

Breakfast   Fresh fruit juice, reconstituted dried fruit, diced fresh fruit
Muesli, porridge
Egg, yoghurt, cheese, meat
Wholegrain bread or toast
Herbal tea or coffee substitute

Lunch   (assuming that it is a packed lunch)
Wholemeal roll, sandwiches, with a variety of fillings e.g. cheese, cottage cheese, salad, fish, meat
Salad, carrot, celery
Fruit
Yoghurt and nuts and raisins (optional)

Evening meal   Small portion of fish, meat with vegetables or rice, meat or vegetable casseroles, egg dishes, pasta dishes
Green or mixed salad
Yoghurt or nuts and raisins (optional)

Try to shop weekly, buying vegetables and fruit twice a week to keep them fresh. If storage facilities will not allow weekly shopping, buy your food in small quantities twice a week and keep all perishables in the fridge, or a dark, cool cupboard.

Certain cooking utensils will help to make life easier in limited circumstances and enable you to broaden your culinary horizons and to do some substantial cooking.

A wok – this Chinese cooking utensil produces crisp, cooked vegetables or tender strips of meat in no time at all, with the minimum of fat, smell and space.

A dry pan – you can cook whole meals in this pan with very little smell, space, time and fuel.

An electric casserole – if you prepare the ingredients the night before, or just before leaving for work, the food can be left cooking on a low heat during the day and will be ready to eat when you come home.

A pressure cooker – you can cook whole meals or a number of vegetables at one time in this versatile utensil. It speeds up the cooking time of hard foods such as pulses and is space saving and highly cost effective.

All these utensils come with a book of instructions and sometimes with recipes, which will allow you to broaden your range of dishes.

Losing Weight
More than one third of Britain's population is overweight, and though there are a variety of reasons for this, the chief reason is that we eat too much, especially of high energy foods, fat and refined carbohydrates. What the body does not burn as energy, it stores as fat.

Being overweight is a form of malnutrition and is as serious as being undernourished, because apart from making us unattractive, it reduces our life expectancy, increases the risk of heart disease, high blood pressure and diabetes, and contributes to dental decay, diverticulitis, constipation and varicose veins.

Large appetites very often stem from being fed cereals too early as a baby. Excess cereals, stored as fat, create a desire for large amounts of food, setting eating patterns for life. As we get older and less active, we compound this problem by eating as much as we ate when we were younger and more active. This is the cause of 'middle-age spread' and is one reason why so many elderly people are overweight.

There is good news, though, and that is that it is never too late to slim. People of any age will begin to feel better within a week or two of dieting.

There are various ways of losing weight. You can follow one of the crash diets advertised in magazines, or use those special 'slimmers' meals on sale in chemists'. There are even pills that swell in the stomach to reduce the appetite, and others that suppress it. But none of these methods is satisfactory or long lasting. The body does not get the nutrients that it needs to function properly and many of these preparations can have serious side effects, including insomnia and high blood pressure. Not only that, but as soon as you stop the diet and eat normally again, you will put on the weight you lost because you have not re-educated your palate to eat the correct foods in the correct quantities. If you diet often, the fluctuations in body weight can damage your health.

Most nutritionists agree that the only safe and effective way to lose weight is to eat less and to eat wholefoods. Wholefoods help to regularise body weight and, by eating them in the correct quantities, the overweight will shed pounds and the underweight will gain them. So it is not so much a diet you need as a new way of eating. Plenty of exercise will help too, if your doctor permits it. Apart from toning up the sagging muscles, exercise speeds up the rate at which your metabolism burns up fat and so it is a valuable slimming aid.

Begin by standing on the scales, recording your weight and then writing down your chest, waist and hip measurements. Find out what your weight should be and note how many pounds you need to lose. As you follow your new eating plan you can weigh and measure yourself at regular intervals. Watching those figures get smaller will encourage you and bolster up any weakening will. You will soon begin to feel fitter, more alert and energetic and these will be added incentives to persevere.

Find the correct calorie (kilocalorie) count for your age and activity group (see Appendix) and subtract 500 calories, so that you will be eating less than your body needs. The body will break down and burn up fatty tissue to make up the calories required.

Then take an honest look at your present diet. Note all those refined and fattening foods which you know do not feed you: sugar, salt, alcohol and beer; convenience foods; snacks such as biscuits, crisps and the like; refined carbohydrates such as white bread and cakes, and pastry made with white flour; then fatty foods, especially those containing animal fat, such as deep fried foods, fatty meats, etc. Aim to give up all these and gradually replace them with wholefoods.

Plan your diet carefully. Follow the advice given in Chapter 9, but stick to the proportions suggested here. Reduce your carbohydrate to 20 per cent of your total daily food intake. Aim to eat one carbohydrate food with each meal and make sure that it is unrefined. Eat wholemeal bread and pastry etc., have muesli instead of sugar-coated breakfast cereals, and baked potatoes instead of chips. Increase your protein intake to 20 per cent. Eat grilled or baked fish and lean cuts of meat or chicken or turkey. Use cottage cheese and skimmed milk, unless you have deficiencies in vitamins A, D and E. Reduce your fat consumption to 10 per cent of your overall daily food and use mostly unsaturated fats such as vegetable oils for cooking, salad oils and soft margarines. Drink plenty of fruit and vegetable juices, and increase your overall intake of fresh fruit and vegetables to 50 per cent of your daily diet. Try to eat much of it raw, to provide bulk and stave off hunger pangs. It will also eliminate waste and help to cleanse your body at the same time.

Try not to eat between meals. But if this is impossible, eat a piece of fruit or a raw carrot, or have five to six small meals a day instead of the usual three.

A raw food day once a week will help you to lose weight more quickly.

When you reach your correct weight, increase your food intake slightly to cover the extra 500 calories your body will now need. But continue with the wholefoods.

Eating for a Healthy Baby
The Health Service provides the prospective mother with a great deal of maternity care, but doctors now realise that there is much that the mother herself can do to have a healthy baby and to stay healthy herself. The best thing that she can do to prepare for pregnancy is by changing to a wholefood diet some months before she plans to conceive, so that all the nutrients the baby needs to develop properly are present in the mother's bloodstream.

Preparing for pregnancy. The foetus develops quickly in the first four months – often before you realise that you are pregnant – and although the foetus is very tiny, by the end of the twelfth week, all the major organs, face and limbs are completely formed. This is when problems can occur if the diet is deficient in the required nutrients.

Examine your diet and start as you mean to go on through pregnancy and beyond. Give up all refined foods and empty calories. Cut out white bread, pastry and cakes, plus white refined sugar and convenience foods, including savoury snacks and fizzy drinks.

Instead, eat a balanced wholefood diet of fresh foods as suggested Chapter 9. Eat a moderate amount of wholemeal bread and pastry. Use brown sugar, honey or molasses as a sweetener, and a little unsaturated fat. Eat plenty of non-starchy protein foods such as fish, liver, pulses, cheese, eggs, yoghurt, wheatgerm and plenty of salads and fresh fruit to provide the protein and vitamins needed during the pregnancy. Eat plenty of dark green vegetables such as spring greens, as they contain folic acid which the foetus needs to develop properly.

If you smoke give this up, if possible, well before you plan to become pregnant, because it can damage the health and development of the baby. Studies have shown that nicotine and carbon monoxide in cigarettes can damage the placenta and prevent the baby from absorbing nutrients efficiently. As a result, the baby is 'starved' and does not grow as well as it might. On average, smokers' babies are about 8.5 oz (approximately 200 g) lighter than other babies and there is the risk of the baby growing up to be shorter and less intelligent than it should be. There is also a greater risk of miscarriage and premature birth among women who smoke.

Alcohol, tea and coffee can also affect the baby's absorption of nutrients through the placenta, so give these up too. Instead, drink fresh fruit and vegetable juices, or the herbal teas recommended in Chapter 8. Raspberry leaf tea is especially good for pregnant women, as it relaxes the muscles of the womb and helps to prepare the body for birth. An equal mixture of wormwood, centaury and blessed thistle also helps to prevent nausea.

Diet during pregnancy. There is a great tendency to eat for two, and so to put on weight, when you become pregnant. This is not necessary for the baby and the extra weight can be difficult to shed after the birth. It also increases the risk of high blood pressure. Instead, doctors recommend that you eat well for one, following a wholefood diet, including some fat, a moderate amount of unrefined carbohydrate, plenty of non-starchy proteins and fresh fruit and vegetables to give the baby the full range of vitamins, minerals, trace elements and essential fatty acids that it needs during the first few months of development. Clinics often provide vitamin and mineral supplements and these should be taken along with a healthy wholefood diet, and not in place of it.

The early months of pregnancy can be quite uncomfortable as the body reacts to the changes going on within it. There can be feelings of irritability, depression, nausea, vomiting, aversions, cravings, heartburn and other digestive problems. A wholesome diet will help, but there are other things that you can take to provide relief. For depression and irritability take a natural vitamin B supplement, such as brewer's yeast or dessicated liver tablets. Chew a few nuts and raisins when you feel sick and eat bland wholefood meals, avoiding heavily spiced or fatty meals. Grill foods rather than frying them, eat plenty of salads without an oil dressing, and use a little, and only a little, butter or soft margarine where necessary in cooking. If you find milk too fatty, eat yoghurt and cottage cheese instead.

Start the meal with a piece of fruit or a salad to get the digestive juices working and prepare the stomach for the food that follows.

Try to avoid all drugs, including aspirin, during pregnancy and breast feeding, unless your doctor insists upon it. These can get into the bloodstream and be passed on to the baby, sometimes with dire consequences. Make sure that you get plenty of exercise, rest, fresh air and sunshine.

Feeding the baby. Most doctors agree that breast feeding is best for mother and child, because the milk is especially suited to the baby's needs. It ensures the correct rate of growth, and contains antibodies which strengthen the baby against infections, such as gastro-intestinal problems and respiratory and middle ear infections, all of which babies are prone to. It also helps to keep the baby feeling comfortable. It has been found that a breast fed baby is less liable to infectious childhood diseases such as whooping cough, and to heart-related diseases and allergies in later life.

Breast feeding benefits the mother, too, by helping the womb and figure to return to normal. It also strengthens the emotional bonds between mother and baby.

Cow's milk is obviously suited to the needs of a fast growing calf, but it contains too much protein, sodium (salt), fatty acid, lactose and vitamin C for the growing human baby. The extra salt in cow's milk can produce enlarged tonsils and catarrhal conditions in babies. If it is impossible to breast feed your baby, use the dried milk feeds which have been carefully prepared to simulate mother's milk and follow the instructions on the container carefully.

Eat the same wholefood diet as you did during your pregnancy, but increase your fluid intake to compensate for the amount of fluid taken by the baby when feeding. Drink up to three pints of milk or fruit and vegetable juices a day. Continue to avoid cigarettes, alcohol, coffee and tea, and also any drugs, as these are in part passed on to the baby through the milk.

Weaning the baby. Breast feeding can go on indefinitely, but the baby can be weaned when it is between four and six months old. Do this gradually, by giving the baby half a teaspoonful of solids such as egg yolk or puréed fruit or vegetables cooked in milk, just before his milk feed. Then around the sixth month introduce him to sieved meat or fish. Do not worry if it is rejected at first; try again in a couple of days and he will soon take the food when he is ready.

Avoid sugar and white flour. Keep the baby off canned baby foods. They are extremely sweet and tend to encourage a taste for sweet foods which can last a lifetime.

When the baby is teething and needs something to chew on, feed him a piece of apple or carrot or a wholewheat rusk. A growing baby will also need extra vitamins, but these are usually supplied by the ante-natal clinic.

Vegetarianism

Strictly speaking, a vegetarian is someone who eats no meat or fish, or products such as gelatine, aspic and lard which are indirectly derived from the slaughter of animals. Most do eat eggs and dairy produce, though, and are known as 'lacto-vegetarians'.

Some vegetarians stick rigidly to a vegetarian diet, others eat vegetarian foods at home but solve their social problems by eating meat and fish when invited out. Many call themselves vegetarians but eat fish and white meat such as chicken.

Vegans, on the other hand, are uncompromising and avoid meat, fish and all animal by-products, including eggs, honey and dairy produce. Although this eliminates a major source of protein, vegans can eat a healthy and balanced diet with the careful use of other protein sources such as pulses, nuts and cereals. But unless foods are skilfully blended, vegans can become deficient in fat-soluble vitamins and the children can suffer from protein deficiency.

Whether as a result of the rising cost of meat, greater awareness of other cultures, or the prompting of conscience, many people have begun to look closely at vegetarianism and to adopt it in part or in full. Many are concerned about the way in which we rear our domestic animals, especially the use of battery farming, and they are also worried by the large quantities of grain used to feed animals which it would be much more efficient to give directly to humans.

It is quite possible to eat a healthy diet without meat or fish. Instead, use alternative protein sources such as dairy produce, pulses, nuts and cereals, and follow the menu plan suggested in Chapter 9.

Eat vegetable and animal protein together to make the most of your protein sources, for example, have lentils and pitta bread, macaroni cheese, bean casserole with a cheese topping. Make sure that you eat a little from each major food group at each meal.

By giving up meat and fish you can reduce your fat intake

by one third. Maintain this level by using vegetable oils, low fat cheeses etc.

Further Reading

Bampfylde, Heather, *Countdown to a Healthy Baby*. Collins 1984.

Holme, Rachael, *Pregnancy and Diet*. Penguin 1985.

Templeton, Louise, *The Right Food for Your Kids*. Century 1984.

Brown, Sarah, *Vegetarian Kitchen*. BBC 1984.

Westberg, Marita, *Eat Well Live Longer*. Quartet 1979.

Smith, Delia, *One is Fun*. Hodder & Stoughton 1985.

12

The Meal as a Family Occasion

One of the things that impresses me about the life of Jesus is how busy he was. He was constantly on the move from town to town, meeting people, teaching them, healing them and comforting them. Yet despite this work load, there is never a hint of rush or tension. True, Jesus missed the odd meal because he was so busy and there were occasions when he was tired (Luke 8.23), but he always spent as much time as necessary with those he met, and worked with a calm confidence. He always found time to pray (Luke 6.12) and also to withdraw from the crowds to be with his disciples, or to eat with friends (Mark 6.32).

I must admit that in the early days after my conversion I begrudged Jesus all this 'free' time. He seemed to be constantly going off with his disciples or to eat with friends and it seemed to me that he was wasting time. I could understand why he took meals with social outcasts – it was a sign of his love and acceptance of them – but why spend so much time with his disciples? If he knew how little time he had left, why not spend more of it with the outcasts so that he could reach more people?

Gradually, though, I realised that he knew exactly what he was doing! Being divine he knew what he had come to do (Luke 4.18–19), but being human he had emptied himself of all his power and depended on God the Father for strength and direction. He was totally obedient to God's will (John 6.38) and was in constant touch with him through prayer. In this way he knew exactly how he was to spend his time and who he had to meet.

The human side of him also needed rest. He believed in the principle of the Sabbath, although he was not legalistic about it as the Pharisees were (Matthew 12.1–14). He knew that man needed a break from his work at least once a week to refresh his mind and body, and time for relaxation during the day. One of Jesus's favourite ways of relaxing was to eat with his disciples and with friends. However, those meals did more than feed and refresh the body; they were an opportunity for Jesus to teach and pass on information. In particular, they were an opportunity for him to strengthen the bonds of love between the apostles and himself. These were the people he was going to use to carry on his work after his ascension, and they needed to know his love very deeply in order to love and serve others. So it was important to leave the crowds regularly and be with his disciples. He knew that the relationships needed to be fed as much as the bodies.

I do not know how the balance in your life compares with that of Jesus, but I know that I fail miserably. Just when I think I have got it all sorted out and have pencilled in plans for free time, life takes off, with me clinging on frantically, in a panic because I have so much to do and so little time to do it in. I become tired and anxious and don't enjoy myself at all, because I would much rather be at home in bed.

Eventually it dawns on me that I have been so busy that I never did take that walk or go to that concert. I know I am not alone in this, because the commonest complaints in Christian circles are crowded diaries and tiredness.

We need not feel guilty if we take time off to withdraw from the world at regular intervals. We need time to rest and to be with God and each other. If we do not, we become irritable or depressed and this can damage our spiritual life and even lead to physical illness. This is not very helpful to God, but it is wonderful material for the Devil, who can use it to sow self-doubt and to undermine our faith and relationships with each other. And the two things that tend to suffer most when we are excessively busy are the family and meals.

The family is under serious threat today. The divorce rate in the United Kingdom is one in three and rising. There is increasing juvenile delinquency, partly because of parental neglect. And families are scattered as people move to other parts of the country to find work.

The church is not protected from this. There is increasing strain and breakdown in Christian families and there are some very lonely people within the church family itself. One of the reasons for this is 'busyness'.

Families are important to God. They were given by him as the basic unit of society for the caring and moulding of us all. It is up to us, as Christians, to realise this and to take steps to strengthen the family bonds against the pressures that attack it. You can never develop proper relationships with people you hardly see, and meals missed or taken 'on the run' only lead to indigestion or illness. It is necessary to shut out the world regularly and to spend time with our family, to give them the love and attention that they need to thrive.

One way of doing this, and of relieving indigestion at the same time, is to reinstate the meal as an important family occasion. It still is in Jewish homes, and this is one reason why their family bonds are so close. Make at least one meal a day a time to be with the family. Save reprimands for another time and use the meal as a time to share news and views and to enjoy each other's company. Linger over the meal and get to know one another again, with Jesus's blessing.

The meal is highly adaptable and can be used to strengthen all types of relationships, to bring parent and child closer together for instance, and husband and wife too. If you have very young children, mealtimes can often be fraught. Children naturally need constant attention and it is not easy to relax when young Nicholas is refusing to eat his cabbage and baby Joanna is decorating the walls with her mashed banana. So, if you do not already do this, why not every now and then feed the small children first, put them to bed, then eat afterwards, at your leisure and in peace.

When you and your husband have a chance to be alone – if, for instance, you have teenage children who are out for the evening – take the opportunity to have a special meal together. Reserve an evening in, just for the two of you and make the meal a special occasion. Dress up, cook your favourite dishes and get out the best china and candles. Turn off the television or radio, put down the newspaper and give each other your full attention. It will be just as much fun, and a lot cheaper, than going out to a restaurant.

The meal is also an ideal opportunity to strengthen relationships with friends and other church members. In some ways the church has become as stratified as the world, and very often families, the elderly and the single seem to live separate existences. As a result, there are many lonely people in the church where there should not be. We are called to love one another and we can only do this if we are involved in each other's lives. As Christians we are all members of the family of God, where everyone, young, old, married and single, is known, loved and cared for. The world should be able to look at Christians and note how much we love one another. And one way we can bring this about is by getting to know each other over a meal.

Hospitality is required of us. It is not just God's way of giving us more to do, it is how he wants us to demonstrate his love – and it works! It is a superb way of introducing the Christian life to the non-Christian, and often a simple meal can speak volumes and be of more use than the most articulate theological treatise. As I well know. Before my conversion this was one of the things that crept up from behind and undermined my strong defence against the main thrust of evangelism. I was tremendously impressed by the simple gesture of acceptance in a Christian home and by the atmosphere of love between the family members.

For the single person there will obviously be many times when you eat alone and it is all too easy to dismiss meals as an inconvenience and sit in front of the television with a carton of yoghurt. You would not do this for others: you would cook a proper meal and take trouble over it. You are no less important. Treat yourself well, cook a simple but appetising meal and eat it at the table. Take your time over it and enjoy it. You will feel much better for it.

Once you have gone to the trouble of re-establishing nutritional mealtimes as important family occasions, enhance the effects of them with an attractive table. This need not be elaborate or expensive; in fact, you can do quite a lot with very little. It is those little touches that count. For instance:

▷ Always lay the table properly before the meal, with each place neatly set. This shows you care and creates an atmosphere of anticipation.

▷ Cover the table with a clean table cloth or decorative table mats and fold the napkins in interesting ways.

▷ Have a pretty centrepiece – a piece of driftwood, dried or fresh flowers in an attractive vase, or perhaps a small basket of beautifully arranged fruit.

▷ Use candlelight for special occasions, and gentle background music to create a relaxing atmosphere. You could combine the candle with the centrepiece by placing a piece of wet oasis on an attractive base, place the candle in the top and arrange flowers and leaves around the base.

▷ Ban packets, bottles and jars from the table. Decant the contents into jugs and pots.

▷ Reduce plasticware to a minimum, except for small children of course, and make more use of china and pottery.

Food itself is a valuable decoration if it is arranged

imaginatively and colourfully on the table. It will also help to stimulate the appetite. There is an infinite number of ways of doing this, but here are just a few:

▷ Arrange contrasting coloured vegetables together, for example, carrots surrounded by green peas or another green vegetable.

▷ Serve the salad in a wooden bowl to contrast the colours.

▷ Serve rolls, hot or cold, in a napkin-lined basket.

▷ Arrange cheeses on a bed of shredded or whole lettuce leaves and garnish with sliced tomato, celery leaves or watercress. You can eat these with the cheese to avoid waste.

▷ Arrange the cheese biscuits in an attractive pattern.

▷ Make sure that the meal is hot, if it is intended to be, and the plate too. There is nothing like tepid food to dull the appetite.

Finally – and this has more to do with organisation than decoration, and is strictly for the mum or host – try to organise your meal so that you can be with the family or company the whole time. Nothing used to irritate me more than being in the kitchen stirring the sauce and listening to the laughter coming from the other room, or catching the end of an interesting conversation when I came in with the pudding.

If possible, try to eat in the kitchen where everything is to hand and you can be in on the fun. If that is not practicable, make sure that the whole meal is ready before serving and press your sideboard or dumb waiter back into service by putting away the ornaments and placing the second course on it so that you do not have to leave the room every five minutes.

RECIPES

Stocks and Soups

STOCKS

Well-flavoured stocks form the basis of really fine soups and casseroles, so, if possible, always have some stock at hand in the fridge or freezer. Stock can be made from leftovers from meals, such as the chicken carcass from a roast, or from meat bones from the butcher, the heads and tails of fish, or vegetables, if you want a vegetable stock.

Meat Stock

2 lb (1 kg)[1] meat bones
1 onion, peeled and diced
1 turnip, peeled and diced
1 carrot, cleaned and sliced
2 sticks celery, cleaned and chopped
2 pints (1.2 litres) water
1 teaspoon each celery leaves, parsley, marjoram, thyme

Place the bones, together with all the other ingredients, in a large saucepan, cover and bring to the boil. Reduce the heat and simmer for 2 hours. Strain the stock and allow it to cool. Skim any fat off the top when it has cooled and freeze what you do not intend to use immediately.

Chicken Stock

Make it in the same way as meat stock, but replace the bones with chicken bones or a carcass. Replace the herbs with ½ teaspoon each sage, parsley, tarragon.

---

[1] The quantities in these recipes are listed in both imperial and metric measurements. Use one or the other as they are not interchangeable.

Vegetable Stock

2 sticks celery, cleaned and chopped
1 onion, peeled and diced
1 carrot, cleaned and diced
1 leek, cleaned and sliced
2 tomatoes, cleaned and diced
3½ pints (2 litres) water
1 tablespoon vegetable oil
1 bay leaf
1 clove garlic, crushed
½ teaspoon fresh or green dried thyme
a pinch of marjoram

Place the prepared vegetables and the oil in a heavy pan and fry them until they are pale and tender. Add the water, bring it to the boil and then simmer for 1½–2 hours in a covered pan. Allow the stock to cool, then strain it and freeze. Alternatively, keep it in the refrigerator for up to 3–4 days.

Fish Stock

2 lb (1 kg) fish bones and skin
2 pints (1.2 litres) water
2 sticks celery, cleaned and diced
1 onion, peeled and sliced
1 leek, cleaned and sliced
1 teaspoon vegetable oil
1 clove garlic, crushed
1 bay leaf
1 tablespoon each parsley or fennel

Place the prepared vegetables and oil in a heavy pan and cook gently until they are pale and soft. Add the fish bones, herbs, garlic and water and bring to the boil, then simmer gently for 1–1½ hours. Allow the stock to cool, strain and then freeze.

SOUPS

Soups are a useful starter to meals, but if served with a salad and wholemeal bread, they make a light and nourishing meal for lunch or supper.

Harvest Soup   Serves 4

2 oz (50 g) pearl barley or wholewheat grain	1 pint (600 ml) chicken stock
2 oz (50 g) butter or soft margarine	1 bouquet garni
1 small onion, finely chopped	4 oz (100 g) Cheddar cheese, grated
4 oz (100 g) walnuts, roughly ground	¾ pint (450 ml) milk
	½ teaspoon French mustard
	1 oz (25 g) flour

Place the grain in a bowl, cover with boiling water and leave to stand for about 1 hour. Melt half the butter in a pan and fry the onion until it is transparent. Add the stock, walnuts, drained grain and bouquet garni. Cover, bring to the boil, then simmer for 1 hour or until the grain is tender. Melt the rest of the butter in a separate pan, stir in the mustard and flour and cook for 2 minutes. Remove the pan from the heat and add the milk gradually. Bring the mixture to the boil gently and simmer for about 3 minutes, stirring continuously. Add the sauce to the grain mixture and stir in the grated cheese. Heat the soup without boiling it and serve hot.

Kidney Soup   Serves 4

8 oz (225 g) kidney, skinned and sliced	1 carrot, cleaned and diced
1¾ pints (1 litre) stock	2 tablespoons vegetable oil
1 onion, peeled and sliced	1 oz (25 g) cornflour
2 sticks celery, cleaned and diced	5 tablespoons milk
	½ teaspoon thyme

Place the vegetables and oil in a heavy pan and cook them until they are pale and tender. Add the chopped kidney, stock and herb. Bring to the boil, then simmer for 2 hours. Sieve or liquidise the soup, blend the cornflour with the milk and add it to the soup. Simmer for a further 20–25 minutes until it is thoroughly heated. Serve hot.

Chilled Bortsch   Serves 4–6

1 lb (450 g) cooked beetroot, skinned and diced
2 pints (1.2 litres) beef stock
¼ pint (150 ml) soured cream or yoghurt
2 tablespoons lemon juice
1 bunch chives, finely chopped
soured cream and chives to garnish

Blend the stock with the cream until it is smooth. Stir in the beetroot, lemon juice and chives. Chill in the fridge for 2–3 hours. Serve in cups with a swirl of soured cream, decorated with chopped chives.
NB This soup can be puréed if you prefer

Pistou Soup   Serves 4

4 oz (100 g) haricot beans, pre-soaked
1 onion, peeled and diced
1 carrot, cleaned and diced
1 potato, scraped and diced
4 oz (100 g) courgettes, washed and sliced
½ lb (275 g) tomatoes, skinned and diced
1½ pints (900 ml) stock
1 oz (25 g) vermicelli
1½ tablespoons vegetable oil
a pinch of raw cane sugar
3 cloves garlic
small bunch fresh basil
2½ tablespoons olive oil
1 tablespoon tomato purée

Rinse the beans, place them in a saucepan, cover with water and bring to the boil. Then simmer until the beans are cooked. Drain them and place on one side. Fry the onion in the oil until it is transparent, then add all the other vegetables and cook for a further 4–5 minutes, stirring often. Mix in the haricot beans and the stock. Bring the mixture to the boil, then reduce the heat and simmer until the vegetables are almost tender. Add the vermicelli, cook for a further 10 minutes, until it is tender and all the vegetables are fully cooked. Add a pinch of raw cane sugar.

Meanwhile crush the garlic and basil together in a pestle and mortar to form a smooth paste. Stir in the oil and tomato purée, then mix into the soup just before serving.

This soup is delicious when eaten with lots of grated cheese and hunks of crusty bread. Make a complete meal of it by serving it with a green salad.

Thickening soups

Puréed soups are often thick enough once the vegetables have been sieved or liquidized. Cream soups can be thickened by adding double cream, or a thin white sauce. Potatoes, dumplings or bread help to thicken soups, and so will a beaten egg if added just before serving. Rice, grains (such as wheat or barley) and lentils add bulk and nutrition and can be cooked with the rest of the ingredients.

Garnishes

Fried croutons; deep-fried onion rings; finely sliced tomato, cucumber or spring onions; swirls of cream; Tabasco or Worcester sauce; grated cheese; freshly chopped herbs; coarsely chopped hard-boiled eggs.

Salads

Chick Pea and Apple Salad   Serves 3–4

4 oz (100 g) chick peas, soaked overnight
2 green eating apples, cleaned, cored and diced
1 medium-sized leek, cleaned and sliced
1 tomato, cleaned and diced
bunch of watercress, rinsed
French dressing
crisp lettuce leaves to serve.

Strain the soaked peas, add fresh water and cook until they are firm but tender, approximately 1–1½ hours. Drain the peas and let them cool. Add the diced apple to the peas, pour over the dressing and mix gently but thoroughly. Add the sliced leeks, tomato and watercress just before serving on a bed of lettuce leaves.

Apple, Celery and Walnut Salad   Serves 4

4 oz (100 g) eating apples, sliced
4 oz (100 g) celery, cleaned and chopped
2 oz (50 g) walnuts, finely chopped
2 fluid oz (50 ml) mayonnaise
1 tablespoon parsley, fresh or green dried
lettuce leaves to serve.

Mix the fruit and celery in a bowl, combine with the mayonnaise and serve on a bed of lettuce leaves. Sprinkle with the parsley and walnuts.

Tomato Salad Serves 4

½ lb (225 g) tomatoes, cleaned and sliced
4 tablespoons fresh basil, rinsed and chopped
French dressing

Arrange the sliced tomatoes decoratively on a plate or dish, sprinkle lightly with the dressing and then sprinkle with the freshly chopped basil. Prepare this dish a few hours before serving to allow the herb to permeate the tomato.

Rice Salad Serves 4

8 oz (225 g) brown rice, long grained
1 pint (600 ml) water
2 sticks celery
½ green pepper
2 tomatoes
8 oz (225 g) cucumber
1 tablespoon onion
1 orange, in segments
2 tablespoons chopped parsley
1 tablespoon each chopped chives and basil
French dressing
1 clove garlic

Rinse the rice thoroughly, add a pint of water and cook over a low heat until the water has been absorbed and the rice is tender. Remove the rice from the saucepan and leave it to cool. Clean and dice the vegetables, rub the inside of a salad bowl with the cut clove of garlic and mix the rice and vegetables together in the bowl. Add the orange segments, herbs and dressing and toss thoroughly. Keep the salad covered at room temperature until you are ready to serve it.

Serve it as a side salad, or make it into a complete meal by adding one of the following: nuts, hardboiled eggs, cold chicken or prawns.

Bean Sprouts, Mushroom and Celery Salad Serves 4

8 oz (225 g) bean sprouts, rinsed
6 oz (175 g) button mushrooms, wiped and sliced
1 large head of celery, cleaned and sliced
2 carrots, cleaned and grated
4 tablespoons French dressing
Garnish: chopped celery leaves, chives and parsley
1 clove garlic

Rub the inside of a salad bowl with the cut clove of garlic. Mix the vegetables and herbs together in the bowl, add the dressing and toss the salad gently. Cover and leave at room temperature until ready to serve.

Bean Salad   Serves 2–3

4 oz (100 g) mixed beans, e.g. chick peas, red kidney beans, flageolet beans	1 eating apple
	2 large carrots
	4 in (10 cm) cucumber
1 heart of celery	1 tablespoon parsley
1 green pepper	4 tablespoons French dressing

Soak and cook the beans until they are firm but tender. Cook the kidney beans separately to avoid staining the other beans red, and boil them hard for ten minutes to destroy the toxins. Drain and allow to cool in the salad bowl. Clean and chop the other vegetables and apple, then add to the beans. Mix in the parsley and dressing and toss thoroughly. Cover and chill before serving.

Green Salad   Serves 4

1 lettuce heart, shredded	1 tablespoon each chives and parsley, chopped
½ cucumber, finely sliced	
1 heart of celery, cleaned and diced	4 tablespoons French dressing
1 bunch watercress, rinsed and removed from the stalks	1 clove garlic

Rub the inside of a wooden salad bowl with the cut clove of garlic. Add all the vegetables and herbs. Toss lightly, but thoroughly. Add the dressing just before serving.

Wild Herb Salad   Serves 2

1 medium-sized potato, boiled and cold	1 tablespoon each chives and parsley, chopped
½ oz (12 g) cucumber	1 clove garlic, crushed
equal parts of yarrow, watercress and dandelion leaves	4 tablespoons French dressing

Dice the potato and cucumber. Clean and shred the herbs. Mix them together in a bowl. Add the garlic to the dressing and pour over the salad just before serving. Toss lightly.

Sprouting Beans

Bean sprouts are a convenient and highly nutritious food, rich in vitamins and minerals, and are useful during the winter when the selection of salad vegetables is more limited. You can buy them ready sprouted from healthfood shops or greengrocers, or make them yourself at home.

When sprouting them yourself, use the smaller beans, such as alfafa, adzuki and mung beans, because they sprout more quickly than the larger varieties. Place 2–3 rounded teaspoons of the beans in a dark glass jar. Rinse the beans and cover the neck of the jar with a piece of muslin, then place the jar on its side in a warm place. Rinse the beans every day to wash away the toxins. The beans will sprout within 2–7 days, depending upon the room temperature and can be used raw in salads or stir-fried as a vegetable.

Sauces and Dressings

SAUCES

Basic White Sauce Makes 1 pint (600 ml)

This recipe provides the basis of many delicious variations which can be used to accompany meat or vegetable dishes.

1 pint (600 ml) warmed milk	2 tablespoons flour
3 oz (75 g) butter or soft margarine	pinch celery salt
	1 teaspoon French mustard

Melt the butter in a small saucepan and sprinkle the flour over it when it foams. Stir and cook gently for 2–3 minutes. Gradually add the milk, stirring continuously to stop lumps forming. When all the milk is added, stir in the salt and mustard and bring the sauce to boiling point. Reduce the heat and simmer very gently for 3–5 minutes, stirring continuously. Serve immediately or, if you do not want to serve the sauce straight away, pour a little melted butter over the top to stop a skin from forming.

With this basic sauce, you can now make a variety of sauces by adding other ingredients.

Cheese Sauce

Add 4–8 oz (100–200 g) grated Cheddar cheese to the cooked sauce. Stir until the cheese has melted.

Herb Sauce

Add a variety of freshly chopped herbs with the milk when making the sauce, e.g. 1–3 tbs dill, tarragon, parsley, mint or basil.

Onion Sauce

Add 1 lb (450 g) peeled and chopped onions, previously fried gently in a knob of butter or soft margarine, with the milk. If you prefer a smooth consistency, liquidise the sauce and then return to the heat and warm thoroughly and serve.

Tomato Sauce

1 14 oz (397 g) tin of tomatoes, chopped	1–2 tablespoons tomato purée
	3 tablespoons vegetable oil
1 large onion, peeled and finely chopped	½ teaspoon Barbados sugar
	1 teaspoon each basil and oregano, chopped
1 large clove garlic, crushed	

Heat the oil in a large saucepan and fry the onion and garlic together until they are soft and transparent. Add the tomatoes and tomato purée. Bring the mixture to the boil and then simmer vigorously, without a lid on the saucepan, for 10–15 minutes to reduce the liquid and give the sauce a purée-like consistency. Add the sugar and herbs and serve hot. Sieve or liquidise the sauce if you want a smooth texture, and return to the heat until it has been thoroughly warmed.

NB This sauce freezes well, so make batches of it and use when required.

Apple Sauce

Serve this sauce with fatty meats such as roast pork.

2 large cooking apples, peeled and cored	4 tablespoons water
	4 tablespoons Barbados sugar
	1 oz (25 g) butter or soft margarine

Dice the apples and place them, together with the rest of the ingredients, in a medium-sized saucepan. Cover and cook gently until the apples are soft. Mash the mixture slightly with a wooden spoon to break up the apple. Alternatively, sieve or liquidise the sauce if you prefer a smooth consistency.

Brown Gravy   Useful for vegetarian roasts

¾ pint (400 ml) hot vegetable stock
1 onion, peeled and chopped
2 tablespoons vegetable oil
1 tablespoon flour
1 clove garlic, crushed
bouquet garni

Fry the onion in the oil until it is brown. Add the flour and continue cooking until that has turned brown too. Then add the stock, garlic and bouquet garni. Simmer gently with the lid off until the flour is cooked and the sauce has reduced to a thicker consistency. Strain before serving.

DRESSINGS

These oil-based dressings will keep well, so make them in large quantities and store them in the fridge, or a cool dark cupboard.

Mayonnaise

1 egg yolk
10 oz (275 g) vegetable oil,
juice of half a lemon
1 teaspoon French mustard

Make sure that all the ingredients are at room temperature before you begin. Beat the egg yolk with a whisk and add the oil drop by drop, whisking continuously. Blend in the mustard and lemon juice, and store in a sterilised jar. Keep in the fridge and use when required.

French Dressing   Ingredients per person

2 tablespoons vegetable oil
2 teaspoons lemon juice
1 clove garlic, crushed
¼ teaspoon celery salt
¼ teaspoon each French mustard and Barbados sugar

Beat the ingredients together and blend thoroughly. Toss the salad in the dressing just before serving. Alternatively, make larger quantities and store in a sterilised screw-topped bottle.

Yoghurt Dressing For those on a low fat diet

3 tablespoons yoghurt
1 teaspoon lemon juice
1 clove garlic, crushed
1 teaspoon parsley

Whisk all the ingredients together and then blend with the salad. This dressing will not keep, and so it should be made fresh each time.

Starters

Cottage Cheese Dip

8 oz (225 g) cottage cheese
2 tablespoons mayonnaise
1 tablespoon lemon juice
1 tablespoon chopped chives
½ teaspoon freshly ground black pepper
2 teaspoons chopped parsley
1 teaspoon mixed herbs, e.g. basil, chervil, tarragon

Sieve the cottage cheese and then blend with all the other ingredients (except the herbs) until it forms a smooth consistency. Stir in the herbs, cover and chill before serving. Serve in a decorative dish surrounded by strips of raw vegetables such as green and red pepper, celery, cucumber, carrot and cauliflower.

Stuffed Tomatoes Serves 4

2 large tomatoes, halved
1 stick celery, finely chopped
1 eating apple, cored and finely chopped
2 spring onions, finely chopped
1 teaspoon mixed herbs, basil, chives and chervil
3 tablespoons mayonnaise
lettuce or watercress

Scoop out the pulp from the tomatoes, leaving hollow cups. Mix the pulp with all the other ingredients and pile the mixture into the tomato cups. Serve on a bed of lettuce or watercress.

Avocado Appetizer   Serves 2

1 avocado pear
2 small tomatoes, ripe and finely diced
2 teaspoons onion, finely chopped or minced
2 teaspoons basil and chervil, freshly chopped
4 teaspoons oil and lemon juice, combined

Halve the advocado lengthwise. Remove the stone and scoop out the flesh, leaving the skin intact. Mash the flesh, and all the other ingredients and mix together thoroughly. Return the mixture to the avocado skins. Garnish with a sprinkling of herbs and serve with strips of thin, hot, buttered wholemeal toast.

Mushrooms on Toast   Serves 3–4

½ lb (225 g) mushrooms, wiped and sliced
1 clove garlic, crushed
1 oz butter or soft margarine
3–4 slices toast

Melt the butter or margarine in a pan, add the mushrooms and garlic and cook until they are tender. Toast the bread, spread with butter and place the mushrooms on top, then serve.

Sunflower Peppers   Serves 4

2 large green peppers
6 oz (175 g) raw potatoes, diced
4 tablespoons sunflower seed kernels
2 tablespoons oil
2 onions, peeled and thinly sliced
2 lbs (900 g) tomatoes, peeled and diced
4 tablespoons canned sweet corn
2 tablespoons sultanas
3 oz (75 g) cheese, coarsely grated
1 teaspoon oregano and basil
2 cloves garlic, crushed

Cut the peppers in half lengthways, remove the seeds and core. Cook the pepper halves in boiling water for 10 minutes, drain and place on one side. Cook the diced potato in boiling water until just tender, and drain. Heat the oil in a small pan and fry the onion and garlic until they are soft and transparent. Add the tomatoes, corn, sunflower seed kernels and sultanas. Cover the pan and simmer until the mixture is fairly thick. Add the green herbs and potato. Spoon the mixture into the pepper halves, sprinkle the grated cheese on top, then place the peppers under a hot grill and cook until the cheese has just melted. Serve immediately.

Italian Noodles   Serves 4

4 oz (100 g) wholemeal noodles	4 oz butter
4 oz (100 g) green noodles	2 oz Parmesan cheese
4 tablespoons fresh basil, finely chopped	2 cloves garlic, crushed

Cook the wholemeal noodles in a pan of boiling water for 10–12 minutes. Add the green noodles 5 minutes later. Meanwhile mix the basil, butter and garlic together to form a paste. Drain the noodles once they are cooked, transfer to a serving dish and add the paste. Toss thoroughly to coat the pasta and serve immediately. Sprinkle with grated Parmesan cheese.

Fish

Stuffed Baked Herrings   Serves 4

4 herrings
1 oz (25 g) wholemeal
   breadcrumbs
½ eating apple, grated
1 tablespoon celery, finely
   chopped
1 tablespoon mixed herbs, chives,
   sage, fennel, dill
melted butter or vegetable oil
wheatgerm

Clean the fish, remove the head and the insides. Rinse thoroughly. Roll the fish in wheatgerm, mix together all the remaining ingredients and pack the fish with this stuffing. Lay the fish in a greased baking dish, brush with oil or melted butter, cover with foil and bake for 20 minutes at 425°F (220°C, Gas mark 7).

Tuna Fish Casserole   Serves 4

2   6½ oz (285 g) tins tuna fish
8 potatoes, scrubbed and sliced
2 stalks celery, cleaned and finely
   diced
2½ fluid oz (60 ml) warmed milk
½ onion, peeled and chopped
   finely
2 tablespoons lemon juice
2 egg whites
3 tablespoons mayonnaise
1 tablespoon butter
nutmeg

Boil the potatoes, drain off the water and mash. Stir in the warmed milk and blend until the potato has a smooth consistency. Add the butter and grated nutmeg. Drain the tuna fish and mash it, then add it to the potato, together with the onions, celery and lemon juice.

Pile the mixture into a greased baking dish. Beat the egg whites until they are stiff, fold in the mayonnaise and spread the mixture over the potato. Bake for 30 minutes at 350°F (175°C, Gas mark 3). Serve immediately.

Tomato Fish   Serves 2

1 lb (450 g) cod	1 clove garlic, crushed
½ lb (225 g) tomatoes, peeled and diced	2 bay leaves
	1 teaspoon basil
½ onion, peeled and finely sliced	
1½ oz (40 g) butter	

Fry the fish in 1 oz (25 g) butter, until it is cooked (about 10 minutes) and then place on one side. Fry the onions and garlic together in ½ oz (10 g) butter until they are soft and transparent. Add the tomatoes and herbs and simmer gently for 10 minutes. Flake the fish and add it to the tomato mixture. Cook on a low heat for 5–8 minutes. Serve hot with green vegetables.

Fish Flan   Serves 4

18 in (20 cm) uncooked pastry shell	1 egg
	1 cup warm milk
8 oz (225 g) cooked haddock or cod, flaked	grated cheese
	1 tablespoon herbs, parsley and fennel
3 tomatoes, skinned and sliced	

Arrange the tomatoes and fish on the base of the flan shell. Sprinkle the herbs over the top. Beat the egg, add the milk, then pour over the fish. Scatter cheese on top. Bake for 30–40 minutes at 350°F (180°C, Gas mark 4).

Fish Italian   Serves 4

4 cod steaks	1 tablespoon chopped parsley
4 oz (100 g) mushrooms, wiped and sliced	1 teaspoon chives, chopped
	1 clove garlic, crushed
¼ pint (150 ml) white wine	1 teaspoon wholemeal flour
1 oz (25 g) butter or soft margarine	vegetable oil
2–3 tablespoons fish stock	chopped parsley to garnish

Clean the fish. Fry the mushrooms, garlic, chives and parsley for a few minutes in the butter. Add the flour and cook for 3 minutes. Gradually stir in the stock and wine and bring the mixture to the boil. Reduce the heat, cover and simmer for 10 minutes. Fry the fish in a little vegetable oil, place it in a shallow, greased dish, pour the sauce over the top and garnish with parsley. Serve immediately.

Poultry

Spanish Chicken   Serves 4–6

1   3 lb (1.4 kg) chicken
2 oz (50 g) bacon, diced
2 oz (50 g) butter
8 oz (225 g) tomatoes, skinned and diced
2 onions, peeled and finely sliced
2 green peppers, deseeded and finely sliced
¼ pint (150 ml) chicken stock
wholemeal flour
chopped parsley for garnishing

Joint the chicken and coat the pieces in the flour. Fry the bacon and place it on one side. Fry the chicken pieces in the butter until they are browned, then put them, together with the bacon, in a greased casserole dish. Add the peppers, onions, stock and tomatoes. Cover and cook gently in the oven for 30 minutes, or until the chicken is tender. Garnish with parsley and serve.

Roast Chicken with Tarragon   Serves 4

1   3 lb (1.4 kg) chicken
½ pint (275 ml) chicken stock
½ oz (10 g) butter
2 tablespoons freshly chopped or green-dried tarragon
Wholemeal flour (optional)

Rub the chicken inside and out with 1 tablespoon tarragon. Place the chicken and the giblets in a casserole dish, add the stock and butter. Roast until the bird is tender. Remove the chicken from the casserole. Place the liquid in a saucepan, add 1 tablespoon tarragon and cook for 10 minutes, adding a little wholemeal flour if the liquid is too thin. Serve this sauce with the chicken.

Chicken Pilaff   Serves 6

1   3 lb. (1.4 kg) chicken
3 pints (1.75 litres) chicken stock
2 oz (50 g) almonds, blanched
3 onions, peeled and sliced
3 oz (75 g) stoneless raisins
1 cup unpolished rice
1 clove garlic, crushed
3 tablespoons butter
1 teaspoon each fresh or dried
   summer savory and tarragon
½ teaspoon fresh or dried thyme
¼ teaspoon cinnamon and paprika

Boil the bird in the stock until it is half tender. Fry the onions and garlic in a little butter until they are soft and transparent. Fry the almonds and raisins lightly. Wash and dry the rice and fry in the butter until it is golden. Put the rice into a deep saucepan, add the onions, almonds, raisins, herbs and spices, place the bird in the centre and cover with 3 cups of stock. Simmer gently until the chicken is cooked and the rice has absorbed all the stock. Transfer the chicken to a warm serving dish and arrange the rice mixture around it. Serve hot.

Chicken Hotpot   Serves 4

4 pieces of chicken
2–3 rashers of bacon, diced
1 onion, peeled and sliced
8 oz (225 g) carrots, scrubbed and
   sliced
8 oz (225 g) shelled peas
4 tomatoes, skinned and sliced
1 lb (450 g) potatoes, cleaned and
   thinly sliced
¼ pint (150 ml) chicken stock
2 oz (50 g) oil
wholemeal flour.

Coat the chicken pieces in the flour and fry in the oil until they are golden brown. Place on one side. Fry the onion until it is soft and golden. Remove from the pan and then fry the potatoes until they are golden brown. Mix the peas, carrots, bacon and tomatoes in a bowl and add the fried onion. Then arrange the chicken, vegetable mixture and potatoes in layers in a greased casserole dish. Pour the stock over the mixture and bake for 1 hour at 375°F (190°C, Gas mark 5).

Herb Chicken Serves 6–8

1 3 lb (1.4 kg) roasting chicken, jointed	1 tablespoon vegetable oil
¼ pint (150 ml) red wine	1 teaspoon each tarragon and thyme, or 6 sprigs each fresh herbs
¼ pint (150 ml) chicken stock	
1 oz (25 g) butter	½ teaspoon dried sage
	cream

Place the herbs in a bowl and add the red wine. Brown the chicken in the melted butter and oil. Grease a casserole dish, transfer the chicken to that, add the stock and wine and bake, covered, for 40 minutes at 400°F (200°C, Gas mark 6).

Place the chicken on a serving dish. Strain the sauce into a small saucepan, boil rapidly for a few minutes to reduce it slightly, add the cream and pour the sauce over the chicken just before serving.

Herb Turkey Serves 10–12

6 lb (2.8 kg) turkey	2 tablespoons rosemary, fresh or dried
½ lemon	
soft margarine for brushing	¼ pint (150 ml) stock

Stuffing

4 oz (100 g) soft margarine	Juice of ½ lemon
4 oz (100 g) wholewheat breadcrumbs	1½ dessertspoon fresh chopped or green-dried parsley;
½ small onion, peeled and finely chopped	½ teaspoon each marjoram, thyme, lemon thyme fresh chopped or green dried
1 clove garlic, crushed	
1 large egg	pinch paprika
grated rind of 1 lemon	

Stuffing: Mix together the herbs, lemon juice, grated rind, onion and garlic. Add the soft margarine and cream well. Then add the egg, paprika, and breadcrumbs and mix together thoroughly.

Turkey: Rub the bird inside and out with the cut lemon, then do the same with the rosemary. Brush the outside of the bird with melted margarine and sprinkle with the rosemary. Stuff the bird with the stuffing mixture and wrap it in buttered foil. Place it on its back in a baking tin and cook in a preheated oven at 400°F

(200°C, Gas mark 6) for 2 hours. Turn the bird half way through cooking, and then 30 minutes before the end remove the foil and turn the bird breast upwards for browning. When it is cooked, pour the juices off into a saucepan, add the stock and heat. Serve this as the gravy.

Roast Duckling with Walnut and Apricot Stuffing Serves 4–6

1 large duck
1 small onion, peeled and quartered

Stuffing
1 onion, peeled and finely chopped
½ small head of celery, finely chopped
2 oz (50 g) soft margarine
6 oz (175 g) dried apricots, diced
1 clove garlic, crushed
4 oz (100 g) seedless raisins, whole
Grated rind and juice of 1 small lemon
Grated rind and juice of 1 orange
6 oz (175 g) walnuts, roughly crushed

Gravy
1 teaspoon wholemeal flour
5 fl oz (150 ml) stock or sherry

Stuffing: Fry the onion and celery in the soft margarine until soft and transparent. Place all the other stuffing ingredients in a small bowl, add the onion mixture and combine thoroughly. Stuff the duck with the mixture.

Place the duck in a roasting pan, together with the quartered onion, and roast for 30 minutes at 400°F, 200°F, Gas mark 6 and then for an hour, or until the duck is tender at 375°F (190°C, Gas mark 5). Test by piercing the bird under the wing – the juices should run clear.

Gravy: Remove all the fat, leaving the dark juices and residues. Decant these into a saucepan and sprinkle with the wholemeal flour. Stir this in thoroughly to prevent the formation of lumps. Gradually add the stock or sherry and stir until the mixture turns brown.

Meat Dishes

Liver Casserole   Serves 4

1 lb (450 g) lambs liver, skinned and sliced thinly
½ lb (225 g) mushrooms, wiped and sliced
1 onion, peeled and chopped
2 carrots, scrubbed and sliced
¼ pint (150 ml) meat stock
1 dessertspoon cornflour
4 tablespoons soy sauce
1 bay leaf
1 teaspoon each parsley, thyme and basil
1 clove garlic, crushed
oil for frying
wholemeal flour

Fry the onions and garlic together until they are soft and transparent. Place on one side. Boil the carrots in a little water until they are partly cooked. Coat the liver in flour and fry briefly to seal in the juices. Grease a casserole dish and place alternate layers of liver, mushrooms, onions and carrot into the dish. Sprinkle the herbs over the meat layer. Combine the cornflour, soy sauce and stock. Pour over the liver and vegetables and bake for 30 minutes in the oven at 350°F (180°C, Gas mark 4). Serve with mashed potatoes and creamed spinach.

Meat Loaf   Serves 4–6

2 lb (900 g) finely minced meat
6 oz (175 g) wholemeal breadcrumbs
1 onion, finely chopped
1 green pepper, deseeded and finely chopped
2 beaten eggs
3 tablespoons vegetable oil
1 teaspoon French mustard
1 teaspoon soy sauce
½ teaspoon each thyme and marjoram
1 teaspoon sage

Mix all the ingredients together thoroughly, except the oil, adding the eggs last. Grease a loaf tin with a little oil and pack in the mixture firmly. Place in the refrigerator for about 1 hour, then turn the loaf out on to a baking tin. Pour the vegetable oil over the loaf and bake for approximately 1 hour at 300°F (150°C, Gas mark 2). Serve with a tomato sauce.

Stuffed Cabbage Leaves　Serves 4–5

1 lb (450 g) minced beef
6 oz (175 g) cooked wholegrain rice
1 medium-sized cabbage, or spring greens
1 onion, peeled and chopped
½ pint (275 ml) meat stock
2 teaspoons cornflour
1 teaspoon coriander, crushed
2 bay leaves
parsley to garnish.

Select the biggest and the best cabbage leaves, wash thoroughly and cook in boiling water for 5 minutes. Drain well. Brown the onion in a little vegetable oil, then place in a bowl, together with the meat, rice and coriander and mix together well. Divide the mixture equally between each cabbage leaf. Roll up the leaves carefully, securing with a toothpick if necessary. Place the stuffed leaves in a greased casserole dish, add the bay leaves and stock and bake in a moderate oven for 45 minutes. Thicken the remaining sauce with a little cornflour, pour the sauce over the stuffed cabbage leaves and garnish with the parsley. Serve with creamed potatoes and steamed carrots.

Rabbit Casserole　Serves 4

4 hind quarters of rabbit
4 oz (100 g) lean bacon, diced
1 rabbit liver, chopped
2 pints (1.1 litres) stock
1 onion, finely chopped
1 clove garlic, crushed
4–6 juniper berries
1 bay leaf
1 teaspoon each lemon balm, rosemary and summer savory
½ teaspoon lemon peel
wholemeal flour
vegetable oil

Fry the rabbit joints briefly in a little oil until they are brown. Add the rabbit liver, garlic and chopped onion. When the meat is well browned, spinkle with flour, stir well and then gradually add the stock, herbs, juniper berries and lemon peel. Cover and simmer on a low heat until the rabbit is quite tender (approximately 1 hour). Serve with noodles or brown rice and a green salad.

Baked Chops   Serves 2

2 large pork chops	1 bay leaf
1 onion, peeled and sliced	¼ teaspoon thyme
5 potatoes, scrubbed and sliced	1 clove garlic, crushed
¼ pint (150 ml) beef stock	vegetable oil for cooking
1½ tablespoons tomato purée	1 clove garlic, peeled

Remove as much fat from the meat as possible and grill the chops for about 2 minutes on each side. Fry the onion and crushed garlic together in a little oil until they are soft and transparent. Rub the inside of a casserole dish with a peeled and cut clove of garlic, grease the dish and line the base with the sliced potatoes. Cover the potatoes with the fried onion and garlic, sprinkle with thyme, add the bay leaf and lay the chops on top. Bring the beef stock to the boil, stir in the tomato purée and pour over the chops. Bake in a hot oven for about 30 minutes at 425°F (220°C, Gas mark 7).

Vegetarian Dishes

Vegetable Casserole   Serves 4

8 oz (225 g) spinach, rinsed and de-stalked
6 oz (175 g) cauliflower, in florets
6 oz (175 g) Cheddar cheese, grated
6 oz (175 g) white cabbage, shredded
2 carrots, scrubbed and sliced
1 onion, peeled and sliced
1 large courgette, sliced
1 red or green pepper, deseeded and sliced
1 oz (25 g) wholemeal breadcrumbs
1 oz (25 g) butter
1 oz (25 g) wholemeal flour
¼ pint (150 ml) milk
¼ pint (150 ml) vegetable stock
vegetable oil for cooking
2 teaspoons curry powder

Cook the spinach in the water clinging to it after rinsing. This will take about 10 minutes. Heat the oil and gently fry the courgette, onion, cauliflower, white cabbage, pepper and carrots for 5 minutes to seal in the flavour. Place these vegetables in an ovenproof dish, with a layer of spinach on top. Melt the butter in a pan, stir in the flour, cook for 2 minutes and gradually stir in the stock and milk. Bring to the boil, reduce the heat and simmer for 2 minutes, stirring continuously. Stir in 4 oz (100 g) of the cheese and the curry powder. Pour the sauce over the vegetables. Mix the breadcrumbs and the remaining cheese together and sprinkle on top of the vegetables. Bake in the oven for about 1 hour at 375°F (190°C, Gas mark 5). Serve hot.

Peanut Paella   Serves 4

4 oz (100 g) peanuts	1 green or red pepper, deseeded and finely sliced
4 oz (100 g) long-grain brown rice, washed	2 tablespoons vegetable oil
1 14 oz (400 g) tin tomatoes, sieved or liquidised	2 cloves garlic, crushed
1 pint (570 ml) vegetable stock	2 teaspoons basil
5 sticks celery, cleaned and diced	½ teaspoon paprika
1 onion, peeled and finely sliced	1 lemon
	1 hard-boiled egg, sliced.

Fry the onion and garlic in the oil for a few minutes until they are soft and transparent. Add the rice, peanuts, basil and paprika and cook for a few minutes, turning constantly to roast the nuts. Mix in the pepper and celery. Pour the stock and liquidised tomatoes on to the mixture, bring to the boil and then simmer, uncovered, for about 40 minutes. Stir regularly. The rice should be cooked by now and all the water absorbed, but add more stock and cook for a while longer if it is not. Garnish with lemon wedges and slices of hard-boiled egg and serve with a green salad.

Bean and Vegetable Stew   Serves 4

8 oz (225 g) black-eyed beans	1 green pepper, cleaned, deseeded and sliced
1 14 oz (400 g) tin of tomatoes, liquidised or sieved	2 cloves garlic, crushed
1 large onion, peeled and thinly sliced	2 oz (50 g) butter
3 sticks celery, cleaned and sliced thinly	1 tablespoon tomato purée
3 carrots, scrubbed and diced	2 tablespoons chopped parsley, fresh if possible.

Soak the beans overnight in water. Drain and rinse, then cook in a saucepan of water until they are tender (about 40 minutes). Drain the beans and place on one side. Heat the butter and add all the prepared fresh vegetables. Fry them gently until they are almost tender. Add the beans, liquidised tomatoes and tomato purée and simmer gently for 10–15 minutes until all the vegetables are tender but crisp. Serve sprinkled with parsley. This dish goes well with creamed potatoes and green beans.

Vegetarian Roast Serves 4

8 oz (225 g) chick peas, soaked the night before
4 oz (100 g) milled nuts
2 eggs, separated
2 slices fresh wholemeal bread
1 onion, peeled and sliced
1 leek, cleaned and sliced
1 stick celery, cleaned and sliced
1 clove garlic, crushed
2 tablespoons parsley
2 tablespoons mixed herbs, e.g. thyme, marjoram, sage and bay leaf
butter and oil for frying
wheatgerm

Rinse the beans and cook in fresh water until they are firm but tender (approximately 1–1½ hours). Dice the bread, cover with boiling water and stir until it dissolves and forms a smooth consistency, then place on one side. Fry the onion and garlic in a little butter and oil until they are golden, then add the leek, celery, parsley and other herbs. Cook for a further few minutes. Add the bread and fry until the water has evaporated. Remove from the heat and allow the mixture to cool. Mash the beans and add to the mixture, together with the milled nuts and the 2 beaten egg yolks. Mix together thoroughly.

Shape the mixture into a loaf, brush with egg white and roll in wheatgerm. Do this several times until it is well coated. Place the loaf into a pan containing a little hot fat and roast for 15–20 minutes at 400°F (200°C, Gas mark 6). Baste frequently. Serve with a brown gravy and roast potatoes, carrots, parsnip and a green vegetable.

Lasagne al Forno Serves 4

8 oz (225 g) spinach, washed and chopped
8 oz (225 g) curd or Ricotta cheese
3 oz (75 g) Mozzarella or Gruyère cheese, grated
1 oz (25 g) Parmesan cheese, grated
1 14 oz (400 g) tin of tomatoes, chopped roughly
8 oz (225 g) white or green lasagne
1 onion, peeled and chopped
½ green pepper, deseeded and finely chopped
2 cloves garlic, crushed
2 eggs, beaten
1 tablespoon parsley, chopped
½ teaspoon each basil and oregano
1 bay leaf
vegetable oil for cooking

Fry the onion and garlic together in the oil until they are soft and transparent. Add the tomatoes, pepper and herbs and simmer gently for 25–30 minutes, adding water if necessary. Mix the spinach with the Ricotta, Parmesan and beaten eggs. Stir in the parsley. Cook the lasagne in boiling water for 10 minutes and drain well.

Grease a shallow square baking dish. Arrange a layer of lasagne in the bottom, spread with some spinach mixture and sprinkle with some Mozarella cheese. Cover with some tomato sauce. Repeat the layers once or twice, finishing with cheese. Cover with aluminium foil and cook in a pre-heated oven for 60 minutes at 350°F (180°C, Gas mark 4). Remove the foil 10 minutes before the end of the cooking time. Serve with garlic bread and a green salad.

Cheese and Lentil Croquettes   Serves 4

12 oz (350 g) split red lentils
6 oz (175 g) grated Cheddar cheese
1¼ pints (700 ml) vegetable stock
1 onion, peeled and finely chopped
½ teaspoon each French mustard, paprika and chilli powder
1 clove garlic, crushed
2 tablespooons oil
1 egg, beaten
1 tablespoon cold water
wheatgerm
wholewheat flour
oil for frying

Wash the lentils several times until the rinsing water is clear. Place them in a saucepan, add the stock and simmer until all the liquid has been absorbed and the lentils are tender. Fry the onion and garlic in the oil until they are soft and transparent. Remove from the heat and add with the cheese, chilli powder, mustard and paprika to the lentils. Mix together thoroughly.

Divide the mixture into 12 or 16 croquettes, roll each one in the wholewheat flour and dip into the beaten egg and water. Then roll in the wheatgerm. Fry the croquettes in hot, shallow oil, turning regularly to brown them evenly and serve hot with a hot tomato sauce, noodles and a mixed salad.

Vegetables

Courgettes Serves 4

1 lb (450 g) courgettes, wiped and sliced
1 large onion, peeled and finely sliced
1 clove garlic, crushed
chopped parsley and chives
vegetable oil and butter for cooking

Fry the onion and garlic in the butter and oil until they are almost transparent. Add the sliced courgettes and cook for a further 5–8 minutes until the courgettes are cooked but still firm. Discard any liquid, mix in the herbs and serve hot.

Ratatouille Serves 4 as a vegetable or 2 as a main dish

This French stew can be eaten hot or cold, or as a main meal in itself, if served with bread and a salad. It also makes an excellent accompaniment to other dishes.

2 large aubergines, diced
2 large courgettes, wiped and sliced
2 large onions, peeled and sliced finely
2 green peppers, deseeded and sliced
6 tomatoes, peeled and finely sliced
8 tablespoons vegetable oil
1 clove garlic, crushed
1 tablespoon parsley
1 tablespoon mixed marjoram, basil, rosemary and lemon thyme

Fry the onions and garlic together in the oil until they are transparent. Add the peppers, aubergines and herbs. Cover and cook for 15 minutes. Then add the courgettes and cook for a further 15 minutes. Add the tomatoes, cover and cook for 40 minutes. If there is too much liquid remove the cover for a while before cooking is complete.

Vegetable Stir-Fry   Serves 4

1 lb (450 g) spring greens, washed and finely shredded
4 oz (100 g) shelled peas
2 oz (50 g) bean sprouts

1 tablespoon vegetable oil
2 tablespoons cider vinegar
2 tablespoons soy sauce
2 teaspoons Barbados sugar.

Heat the oil in a large skillet or wok, add the spring greens, bean sprouts and peas. Stir vigorously for 3 minutes. Mix together the soy sauce, sugar and vinegar. Pour over the vegetables and cook on a high heat for a further minute. Serve immediately.

Chive Potato Cakes   Serves 4

4 medium-sized potatoes, boiled
1 egg, beaten
2 tablespoons butter or soft margarine

1 tablespoon chives, chopped
butter and oil for cooking

Mash the potatoes whilst they are still hot. Add the butter and chives and mix thoroughly. When the mixture has cooled, mix in the beaten egg. Shape into flat cakes and fry in a mixture of oil and butter. Serve hot.

Swede Croquettes   Serves 4

1 lb (450 g) swede
12 fluid oz (330 ml) milk
1 oz (25 g) butter or soft margarine
1 small egg, beaten

3 tablespoons chopped chives
2 tablespoons wholemeal flour
1 egg white
4 oz (100 g) wheatgerm or wholemeal breadcrumbs
vegetable oil for frying

Peel and finely slice the swede and place in the saucepan with the milk. Bring to the boil, then simmer uncovered until the swede is tender (approximately 10–15 minutes) and most of the milk has been absorbed. Drain off any excess liquid. Mash the swede and mix in the butter, chives, beaten egg and flour. Chill the mixture until it is firm. Shape the mixture into croquettes, dip each one in egg white and roll in wheatgerm or breadcrumbs. Fry in shallow oil for about 5 minutes, turning regularly, until they are crispy brown on the outside and heated through to the centre. Serve hot.

Glazed Carrots   Serves 4

1 lb (450 g) carrots, scrubbed and sliced	juice of 1 lemon
2 tablespoons honey	1 tablespoon parsley
	¼ pint (150 ml) vegetable stock

Bring the stock to the boil, add the carrots and simmer until they are crisp but tender. Drain away the liquid and toss the carrots in the honey, lemon juice and parsley. Serve hot.

Buttered Spinach   Serves 4

2 lb (900 g) spinach	¼ teaspoon freshly grated nutmeg
½ oz (10 g) butter or soft margarine	fried croûtons of bread

Rinse the spinach thoroughly, shake off excess water and cook over a gentle heat for 6–8 minutes in the water clinging to the leaves. Drain off any liquid. Melt the butter in a pan, add the nutmeg, then the spinach and coat it thoroughly. Turn the spinach out on to a warm serving dish and surround with croûtons of bread. Serve hot.

Puddings and Desserts

Chocolate Pudding

1 pint (570 ml) milk
1 oz (25 g) carob powder
3 level tablespoons cornflour

2 level tablespoons sugar
a few drops of vanilla essence
grated carob bar for decoration

Mix the cornflour and the carob powder to a smooth paste with a little cold milk. Bring the rest of the milk to the boil, pour over the cornflour mixture and stir well. Return to the pan and heat gently, until the cornflour is cooked. Stir continuously to maintain a smooth consistency. Add the sugar and vanilla essence. Pour into a wet mould. Allow the pudding to cool before chilling in the fridge. Turn out on to a serving dish when set and decorate with grated carob. Serve with cream or yoghurt.

Baked Bananas   Serves 4

4 bananas, peeled and sliced
   lengthwise
juice of 1 lemon

juice of 1 orange
2 teaspoons honey

Place the bananas in a greased shallow, ovenproof dish. Combine the juices and honey, pour over the bananas and cook in a moderate oven for 15–20 minutes. Serve hot with cream or yoghurt.

Crème Caramel

1 pint (570 ml) milk
3 eggs, beaten
¼ pint (150 ml) water

4½ oz (125 g) caster sugar
a few drops of vanilla essence

Place the water and 4 oz (100 g) sugar in a small pan. Heat without stirring until the mixture turns a rich caramel colour. Pour this quickly into a hot, wet mould and coat the inside thoroughly. Meanwhile, place the milk and remaining sugar in a pan and heat to blood heat. Remove from the heat, stir in the vanilla essence and the beaten egg and strain the mixture into the mould. Place the mould in a shallow tin of water and bake in the oven for about 1 hour at 325°F (160°C, Gas mark 7). Leave the pudding in the mould until it is quite cold, then turn out on to a serving dish.

Rice Pudding

2 oz (50 g) short grain brown rice
1½ oz (40 g) Barbados sugar
1½ pints (900 ml) milk
grated nutmeg

Wash the rice and then place it in an ovenproof dish with the milk and sugar. Leave to soak overnight. Sprinkle nutmet over the top and bake in the oven for 2–3 hours at 300°F (150°C, Gas mark 2). Stir once or twice for the first hour, then leave undisturbed until it is cooked.

Fresh Fruit Salad

2 dessert pears, cored and sliced
1 dessert apple, cored and finely sliced
1 orange, peeled and segmented
3 dessert plums, stoned and halved
1 peach, stoned and finely sliced
4 oz (100 g) white and black grapes, halved
1 banana, sliced
a few cherries, stoned and halved
juice of 2 lemons

Toss the apple in half the lemon juice to prevent discoloration. Mix all the fruit in a salad bowl, pour over the remaining juice and serve.

Vanilla Cheesecake

12 oz (350 g) curd or cottage cheese
6 oz (175 g) digestive biscuits, finely crushed
3 oz (75 g) butter or soft margarine
2 eggs, beaten
1 oz (25 g) raw cane sugar
10 fl oz (275 ml) soured cream
vanilla essence
lemon peel for decoration

Melt the butter in a pan, mix in the biscuit crumbs and combine well. Press the crumb mixture into a shallow ovenproof dish about 9 in (23 cm) in diameter and set in the fridge. Sieve the cheese and beat until it is soft. Stir in the beaten eggs, sugar, vanilla essence and cream and mix to a fine consistency. Pour on to the biscuit base and cook in the oven for 30–35 minutes at 350°F (180°C, Gas mark 4). Decorate with grated lemon peel and serve cold.

Breakfast Dishes

Pancakes Makes 6

½ pint (275 ml) milk
3 oz (75 g) wholemeal flour, plain
1 oz (25 g) skimmed milk powder
1 egg, beaten
1 dessertspoon bran
1 tablespoon sesame seeds
pinch of cinnamon
vegetable oil

Mix all the ingredients together, with the exception of the oil. Grease a skillet with a little vegetable oil and spoon in a little of the batter to cover the base of the skillet. Cook on both sides, and repeat the process until you have used all the batter. Keep the pancakes warm under the hotplate. These pancakes can be made the night before if preferred, and heated up the next day.

Muesli Mix

1 lb (450 g) rolled oats
4 oz (100 g) wheatgerm
2 oz (50 g) bran
2 oz (50 g) sesame seeds
4 oz (100 g) sunflower seeds
2 oz (50 g) almond niblets
2 oz (50 g) soya flour
2 oz (50 g) skimmed milk powder
8 oz (225 g) currants

Place the oats, bran and nuts in an ovenproof dish, and bake in the oven until the ingredients have turned a light golden colour. Stir regularly to prevent burning. Remove from the oven, mix in the rest of the ingredients. Allow to cool and then store.

Banana Ambrosia   Serves 2–3

2 bananas, mashed until frothy
2 apples, chopped or grated
2 dessertspoons natural yoghurt
2 dessertspoons rolled oats
1 dessertspoon wheatgerm
1 dessertspoon bran
2 teaspoons pure fruit juice

Mix the ingredients together and serve.

Liquid Breakfast

Take this as a food supplement if you feel that you need it, or as a breakfast if you are in a hurry.

½ pint (275 ml) milk
2 dessertspoons skimmed milk powder
1 egg, beaten
4 tablespoons pure fruit juice
½ banana, mashed
1 dessertspoon bran
1 dessertspoon wheatgerm
1 dessertspoon yoghurt
1 teaspoon vegetable oil

Mix all the ingredients together thoroughly. Store in a sterilised bottle in the fridge and drink a wineglassful as a supplement, or two glassfuls as a breakfast.

Packed Lunches

Pasties Makes 4–6

13 oz (375 g) wholemeal pastry
8 oz (225 g) potatoes, scrubbed and diced
1 small onion, peeled and sliced finely
12 oz (350 g) minced meat
4 tablespoons soy sauce
milk to glaze

Fry the potato and onion in a little oil for 3–4 minutes. Remove with a slotted spoon and place on one side. Fry the meat quickly to seal it, then mix with the potato and onion. Add the soy sauce and allow to cool. Roll out the pastry thinly on a floured surface and cut out 4–6 rounds with a circular cutter. Divide the filling between the rounds, brush the edges with milk and press together with the fingertips. Place the pasties on a greased baking sheet, brush with milk and prick the sides with a sharp knife. Bake for 25–30 minutes at 400°F (200°C, Gas mark 6), until they are a golden brown.

Vegetarian Pasties

In place of the meat in the above recipe you can use the equivalent weight of cheese, beans, mushrooms, or other vegetables, either separately or in combination.

Quiche Lorraine

8 oz (225 g) wholemeal pastry	1 garlic, crushed
3 oz (75 g) Cheddar cheese, grated	vegetable oil for cooking
2 eggs, beaten	¼ pint (150 ml) milk
1 onion, peeled and finely chopped	2 tomatoes, skinned and sliced
	1 tablespoon parsley and chives, chopped

Roll out the pastry on a floured surface and line a greased fluted flan dish 8½ in (21 cm) in diameter. Strew the base with uncooked beans and bake blind in the oven for 20 minutes at 400°F (200°C, Gas mark 6). Meanwhile fry the onion and garlic in a little vegetable oil until they are soft and transparent. Remove the flan shell from the oven and let it cool a little. Line the base with all but three of the tomato slices, spread the onion and garlic mixture over that and then sprinkle with half the grated cheese. Mix together the eggs, milk and green herbs, pour over the flan mixture and then sprinkle over it the rest of the cheese. Arrange the three remaining tomato slices on top and bake in the oven for about 30–40 minutes at 375°F (190°C, Gas mark 5), or until the filling has set.

You can either bake one large quiche and take slices of it to work with you, or make three or four individual ones, using the same quantities. You can also vary the vegetables according to the season and produce an infinite number of variations on this basic theme.

Vegetarian Scotch Eggs

6 hard-boiled eggs	1 tablespoon chopped parsley
8 oz (225 g) red split lentils	1 beaten egg
¾ pint (400 ml) water	1 teaspoon thyme
1 onion, peeled and minced	*To finish*:
1 clove garlic minced	2 beaten eggs
4 oz (100 g) wholewheat breadcrumbs	wholewheat flour
	wheatgerm
1 tablespoon tomato purée	oil for deep frying

Wash the lentils thoroughly several times and cook in the water until they are tender and all the water has been absorbed.

Meanwhile fry the onion and garlic in the vegetable oil until they are soft. Add the lentils, together with the beaten egg, breadcrumbs, tomato purée and herbs. Mix together thoroughly. Let the mixture cool. Shell the eggs and then dip them first in the flour, then in the beaten eggs. Press some of the lentil mixture around the eggs until they are completely covered. Dip the covered eggs into the beaten egg again and roll them in the wheatgerm. Deep fry in hot fat until they are crisp and golden brown. Drain and allow to cool.

Cottage Cheese Triangles

2 large potatoes boiled,	1 oz (25 g) butter
3 oz (75 g) cottage cheese	1 tablespoon soya flour
1 oz (25 g) Cheddar cheese, grated	½ teaspoon each basil and paprika
2½ oz (60 g) plain wholemeal flour	

Mash the potatoes to a smooth consistency and add all the other ingredients, with the exception of the basil and grated cheese. Mix thoroughly to make a firm paste. Place in the fridge for ½ hour to firm up and then roll the mixture out on a floured surface. Roll out several times and fold together again. Finally roll out to ¼ in (0.5 cm) thick and cut into 3 in (7.5 cm) squares. Sprinkle with cheese and basil, fold into triangles, press the edges together firmly and bake in the oven for 30 minutes at 425°F (220°C, Gas mark 7).

Further suggestions for packed lunches

▷ A slice of bean loaf, or a slice of meat loaf with a mixed salad.

▷ Slices of cold meat, a piece of fish, or pâté, or Cheddar cheese, served with a salad.

▷ A thermos flask of thick hot soup.

▷ Then there are sandwiches. These are highly versatile and convenient, but tend to be rather tedious and unappetizing if they are continually served up with cheese or ham fillings. Therefore vary them a little so that sandwiches can become more exciting and realise their full value.

▷ Vary the bread. Use wholemeal, rye bread such as pumpernickel, herb bread, soda bread, pitta bread, etc.

▷ Vary the fillings, too, with fish, salad, a variety of pâtés, meat, and spreads made from beans or cheese.

▷ Cottage cheese, cream cheese or curd cheese can be varied with additions such as finely chopped red and green peppers, crushed garlic, minced onion, fruit (e.g. minced pineapple), nuts, tomato purée, chopped herbs (e.g. parsley and chives), grated carrot or chopped celery.

Further Reading

Hunt, Janet, *The Wholefood Lunch Box*. Thorson's 1983.

Drinks

Lemon Drink

Add the juice of 1 lemon to a glass of chilled water. Sweeten with honey or sweet cicely.

This recipe is suitable for all citrus fruits. You can save time by squeezing a number of fruits and storing the juice in screw top bottles in the fridge.

Ginger Beer

1 oz (25 g) bruised fresh ginger	a few cloves
1 lb (450 g) raw cane sugar	1 tablespoon yeast, ready prepared
2 sliced lemons	1 gallon (4.5 litres) boiling water

Place the sugar in a large bowl, pour the boiling water over it and add the ginger, lemons and cloves. Cover and leave to cool, then add the prepared yeast. Cover again and leave overnight. Strain and bottle in sterilised containers. This is ready to drink at once.

Raspberry Milkshake

2 oz (50 g) raspberry juice
1 teaspoon honey
2 pints (1.1 litres) cold milk

Blend the ingredients together. Chill and then whisk vigorously just before serving, to form a froth.

This recipe is suitable for any soft fruit that is available.

Minted Fruit Cup

1 pint (570 ml) apple juice
juice of 4 large oranges
juice of 4 large lemons
sprigs of bruised fresh mint
honey to taste
Slices of lemon, orange and apple

Place the washed and bruised mint in a jug, add the orange and lemon juice. Cover and infuse for 2 hours. Add the apple juice, together with the honey, stir well and serve chilled. Garnish with the sliced fruit.

Spiced Apple Juice   An ideal winter drink.

1 pint (570 ml) apple juice or cider
1 orange
1 oz (25 g) demerara sugar
3 cloves
1 whole allspice berry
¾ teaspoon grated nutmeg
cinnamon stick servers

Pare the rind thinly from the orange and place in a pan with the apple juice and spices. Bring the mixture to the boil, remove from heat, cover and infuse for 2 hours. Strain the juice and return to the pan, add the orange juice and sugar, place over a low heat and stir until the sugar has dissolved. Serve hot in tumblers with cinnamon stick servers.

Elderflower Champagne

This fragrant sparkling drink is non-alcoholic and can be made from fresh or dried elderflowers.

6 oz (175 g) dried elderflowers (or 4 large flower heads)
1½ lbs (700 g) white sugar
2 tablespoons white vinegar
1 lemon, sliced
1 gallon (4.5 litres) cold water

Place all the ingredients in a large plastic or enamel bowl or bucket. Cover and infuse for 24 hours. Strain and bottle in sterilised screw top bottles and store in a dark place to ferment for 9–21 days, depending on the room temperature. Serve chilled.

Bread, Scones and Pastry

Wholemeat Bread   Makes 2 lbs (900 g) of bread

1½ lbs (700 g) plain wholewheat flour
¾ pint (400 ml) warm water
1 oz (25 g) fresh yeast
4 teaspoons vegetable oil
1 teaspoon salt
1 teaspoon honey

Mix the honey, warm water and yeast together and leave in a warm place for 10 minutes until it is frothy. Mix the flour, salt and oil in a large bowl, make a well in the centre and pour in the yeast mixture. Combine until the mixture forms a dough. Knead the dough on a floured surface for about 10 minutes until it becomes smooth and elastic. Place the dough in a greased bowl, cover and leave it to double in size in a warm place. Knock back and knead for a further 10 minutes, then divide the dough equally and place in 2 greased 1 lb (450 g) loaf tins. Cover and leave the dough to double in size, then bake in a preheated oven at 425°F (220°C, Gas mark 7) for 30 – 35 minutes. Turn out of the tins and cool on a wire rack.

Soda Bread with Herbs   You can make this tasty bread when you are in a hurry.

8 oz (225 g) wholewheat flour
7 oz (200 g) plain white flour
½ oz (10 g) wheatgerm
½ oz (10 g) bran
2 oz (50 g) Cheddar cheese, grated
2 large onions, finely chopped
2 sticks celery, finely chopped
2 teaspooons bicarbonate of soda
2 teaspoons lemon juice
½ pint (275 ml) less 4 tbs milk
1 oz (25 g) butter or soft margarine
2 tablespoons parsley, chopped
1 teaspoon mixed herbs
1 teaspoon salt
milk for glazing

Sieve the flours, bran, wheatgerm, salt and bicarbonate of soda into a mixing bowl and rub in the butter. Add the chopped onion, celery and herbs and mix thoroughly. Combine the milk and lemon juice and mix with the other ingredients to make a soft dough.

Knead the dough lightly on a floured surface, shape into a 9 in (22 cm) round and place on a greased baking tray. Score the round into 8 segments, brush with milk and sprinkle the cheese over the top. Bake in a preheated oven at 400°F (200°C, Gas mark 6) for 30–35 minutes, or until the bread is well risen and golden brown. This bread is best eaten oven-fresh.

Wholewheat Scones   Makes 8–10 scones

8 oz (225 g) wholewheat flour
1 teaspoon bicarbonate of soda
3 oz (150 g) natural yoghurt
2 oz (50 g) soft margarine
milk for glazing

Place the flour and bicarbonate of soda in a bowl and rub in the margarine. Add the yoghurt and mix until a soft dough is formed. Roll the dough out on a floured surface to a thickness of 1 in (2.5 cm) and cut into rounds, using a 2 in (5 cm) circular cutter. Place the rounds on a greased baking tray and brush with milk. Bake in a preheated oven at 400°F (200°C, Gas mark 6), for 10–15 minutes until the scones are well risen and golden. Cool on a wire rack.

Wholewheat Pastry   Ideal for pie toppings and flan cases.

8 oz (225 g) plain wholewheat flour
4 oz (100 g) soft margarine
3 fluid oz (75 ml) cold water
1 teaspoon oil

Make sure that all the ingredients and utensils are cold, then place the flour and margarine in a mixing bowl and work in the fat with a fork until the mixture forms fine breadcrumbs. Make a well in the centre, stir in the oil and water and leave to rest for 5 minutes. Then briefly bring the pastry together with the fingertips. Roll out on a floured board as required.

Crumble

1 oz (25 g) plain wholewheat flour
1 oz (25 g) wheatgerm
1 oz (25 g) soya flour
2 oz (50 g) soft margarine
2 oz (50 g) raw cane sugar

Mix the flour, wheatgerm and soya flour together in a mixing bowl and rub in the fat. Add the sugar and rub between the fingers until the mixture turns into fine breadcrumbs. Use as required.

This can be made in bulk and kept in the freezer to use as a topping for fruit crumbles.

Cakes and Biscuits

Banana and Walnut Loaf

8 oz (225 g) wholemeal self-raising flour
1 lb (450 g) bananas, mashed
1 oz (25 g) soya flour
2 eggs, lightly beaten
2 oz (50 g) chopped walnuts
2 oz (50 g) raw cane sugar
2 oz (50 g) soft margarine
3 oz (75 g) honey
2–3 nuts for decoration

Cream the margarine and sugar together in a bowl until it is light and fluffy. Beat in the honey and eggs. Add the mashed banana and chopped nuts and sieve in the flours. Mix well. Spoon the mixture into a greased 2 lb (900 g) loaf tin, decorate with the walnuts and bake in a preheated oven for 1¼ hours at 350°F (180°C, or Gas mark 4). Turn out the loaf and cool on a wire tray. This keeps well and is delicious served with butter.

Spiced Apple Cake

12 oz (350 g) wholewheat flour
1 lb (450 g) cooking apples, peeled, cored and diced
6 oz (175 g) soft margarine
6 oz (175 g) raw cane sugar
6 oz (175 g) chopped dates
4 oz (100 g) chopped walnuts
2 oz (50 g) raisins
1 teaspoon bicarbonate of soda
3 tablespoons milk
1 teaspoon powdered cinnamon
½ teaspoon each ground mace and nutmeg
juice of half a lemon

Topping:
1 tablespoon raw cane sugar
½ teaspoon ground cinnamon
1 oz (25 g) whole walnuts

Place the apples in a pan with 4 tablespoons of water and the lemon juice, cover and simmer gently until they are soft. Mash the pulp with a wooden spoon and place the apples on one side to cool.

Cream the sugar and margarine together until light and fluffy. Sieve in the flour, bicarbonate of soda and spices. Mix together and then add the raisins, dates, milk and walnuts. Spoon the mixture into a greased 2 lb (900 g) loaf tin, sprinkle with the topping ingredients and bake in a preheated oven for 1¼ – 1½ hours at 325°F (170°F, Gas mark 4). Let the cake cool in the tin for 15 minutes before turning it out on to a wire tray.

Carrot and Apple Muffins

5 oz (150 g) wholewheat flour
1 oz (25 g) skimmed milk powder
1½ teaspoons baking powder
2 eggs, beaten
2 oz (50 g) grated carrot

2 oz (50 g) grated apple
6 oz (175 g) honey
4 fluid oz (100 ml) vegetable oil
¼ teaspoon each ground nutmeg, allspice and cinnamon
½ teaspoon vanilla essence

Sieve the flour, baking powder, milk powder and spices into a mixing bowl. Add the oil, eggs, honey and vanilla essence and mix together gently, but thoroughly. Fold in the carrot and apple. Spoon the mixture into 16 greased patty tins and bake in a preheated oven for 20 minutes at 400°F (200°F, Gas mark 6), until the muffins are firm and well risen.

Flapjacks

6 oz (175 g) rolled oats
1 oz (25 g) bran
1 oz (25 g) wheatgerm
4 oz (100 g) soft margarine

4 oz (100 g) raw cane sugar
2 oz (50 g) sesame seeds
vanilla essence

Melt the butter and sugar in a saucepan. Add the oats, bran, wheatgerm, sesame seeds and vanilla essence. Mix together thoroughly. Spread the mixture in a greased shallow dish and press down well. Bake in a preheated oven for 25–30 minutes at 375°F (190°C, Gas mark 5) until golden brown. Cut into 18 bars and allow to cool in the tray before removing.

Orange and Date Oat Squares

6 oz (175 g) rolled oats
4 oz (100 g) wholewheat flour
5 oz (150 g) Barbados sugar
4 oz (100 g) soft margarine

8 oz (225 g) dates, chopped
juice of 1 orange
grated orange rind

Measure the orange juice and add enough water to make it up to 4 fluid oz (100 ml). Place the dates, orange rind and orange juice in a pan and cook the dates gently until they are soft and pulpy.

Meanwhile blend the margarine with the rest of the ingredients and place half of the mixture over the base of a greased 7 in (18 cm) square tin. Spread the date mixture over that, sprinkle the remaining oat mixture on top and press down lightly. Bake for 35–40 minutes at 350°F (180°C, Gas mark 4). Allow the biscuit to cool in the tin and cut into 16 squares.

Sweet Oatmeal Biscuits

2 oz (50 g) plain wholewheat flour
2 oz (50 g) rolled oats
4 oz (100 g) soft margarine

2 oz (50 g) nuts, finely chopped
1 oz (25 g) Barbados sugar

Cream the margarine and sugar together in a bowl until it is light and fluffy. Stir in the oats and flour and shape the dough into a roll about 1½ in (4 cm) in diameter. Coat with nuts. Wrap the dough in plastic film or foil and chill in the fridge until it is firm. Cut the roll into ¼ in (0.5 cm) thick slices, place on an ungreased baking sheet, prick lightly with a fork and bake for 12–15 minutes at 350°F (180°C, Gas mark 3) or until the biscuits are lightly browned. If they are not crisp, put them back into the oven for a couple of minutes and then cool on a wire tray.

Yoghurt and Cream Cheese

Yoghurt

This recipe is for those without a yoghurt maker.

1 pint (570 ml) milk
2 tablespoons skimmed milk
  powder
1 teaspoon natural yoghurt

Bring the milk to the boil and then let it cool to blood heat. Stir in the powdered milk and natural yoghurt and then pour into sterilised containers. Keep in a warm place until the yoghurt has set. This will take between 4–8 hours, depending on the warmth of the chosen spot. Then keep it in the fridge, where it will firm up even more.

For your next batch, use some of this batch as your starter.

Cream Cheese

Pour 1 pint milk (570 ml) into a basin, cover and allow it to turn into curds and whey. Line another basin with a clean piece of muslin cloth, about 18 inches square and gently pour the separated milk solids into it. Gather up the corners, tie together and hang the solids up to drip, placing a basin underneath to catch the drips. When the solids have stopped dripping and the cheese is firm, remove from the cloth, sieve, and work in a knob of butter. Store in a container and keep in the fridge. The whey makes a refreshing drink, although it can be an acquired taste.

Appendix

Recommended daily amounts of food energy and some nutrients for population groups in the United Kingdom.

Age range[a] years	Occupational category	Energy[b] MJ	Energy[b] Kcal	Protein g
Boys				
under 1		–	–	–
1		5.0	1200	30
2		5.75	1400	35
3–4		6.5	1560	39
5–6		7.25	1740	43
7–8		8.25	1980	49
9–11		9.5	2280	57
12–14		11.0	2640	66
15–17		12.0	2880	72
Girls				
under 1		–	–	–
1		4.5	1100	27
2		5.5	1300	32
3–4		6.25	1500	37
5–6		7.0	1680	42
7–8		8.0	1900	47
9–11		8.5	2050	51
12–14		9.0	2150	53
15–17		9.0	2150	53
Men				
18–34	Sedentary	10.5	2510	63
	Moderately active	12.0	2900	72
	Very active	14.0	3350	84
35–64	Sedentary	10.0	2400	60
	Moderately active	11.5	2750	69
	Very active	14.0	3350	84
65–74	Assuming a	10.0	2400	60
75+	sedentary life	9.0	2150	54
Women				
18–54	Most occupations	9.0	2150	54
	Very active	10.5	2500	62
55–74	Assuming a	8.0	1900	47
75+	sedentary life	7.0	1680	42
Pregnancy		10.0	2400	60
Lactation		11.5	2750	69

Notes

a Since the recommendations are average amounts, the figures for each age range represent the amounts recommended at the middle of the range. Within each age range, younger children will need less, and older children more, than the amount recommended.

b Megajoules (10^6 jules). Calculated from the relation 1 kilocalorie = 4.184 kilojoules, that is to say, 1 megajoule = 240 kilocalories.